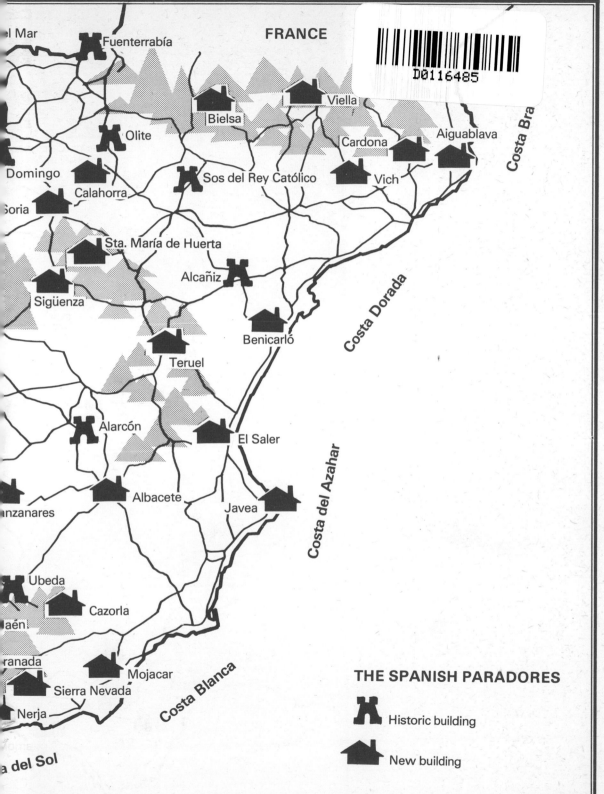

el Mar
Fuenterrabía

FRANCE

D0116485

Bielsa
Viella

Olite
Cardona
Aiguablava

Costa Bra

Domingo
Sos del Rey Católico
Vich

Calahorra

Soria

Sta. María de Huerta

Alcañiz

Sigüenza

Benicarló

Teruel

Costa Dorada

Alarcón

El Saler

Albacete
Javea

Manzanares

Costa del Azahar

Ubeda
Cazorla

Jaén

Granada
Mojacar

Sierra Nevada
Costa Blanca

Nerja

THE SPANISH PARADORES

Historic building

New building

a del Sol

Paradores of Spain

THEIR HISTORY, COOKING AND WINES
JAN READ & MAITE MANJÓN

MASON / CHARTER   NEW YORK 1977

Half-title page: A corridor in
the Parador of the Via de la
Plata before reconstruction.
Title page: The Parador of the
Castillo de Monzón.

Acknowledgments

The authors wish to thank the Ministerio de Información y
Turismo for its generous help, without which it would have been
impossible to write this book. We are particularly indebted to Don
Ignacio Aguirre Borrell, Subsecretario de Turismo; Don José
Antonio Ferreiro Piñero, Director de Administración Turistica
Española; and also Don Juan Sánchez Lorenzo and Don Rafael
Ernesto Gonzalez of the Public Relations section of the Ministry.
We also received every encouragement from Don Manuel Fraga
Irribarne, formerly Spanish Ambassador in London, and Don
Francisco Mayans of his staff at the time. The Administrators of
the Paradores and Albergues, who welcomed us so warmly, are too
numerous to mention by name.

First published 1977 by
Macmillan London Limited
First published in the United States by
Mason/Charter Publishers

ISBN: 0-88405-495-0

Printed in Great Britain

Contents

Foreword

Towards the beginning of *Don Quixote* Cervantes describes how the Knight of the Sorrowful Countenance rode out in search of errantry and adventure. 'He travelled all day, and at nightfall he and his steed were tired and dead of hunger; and looking in all directions for some castle or abode of shepherds where they might eat and rest their weary bodies, he saw, not far from the road, an inn. It was as if a star had shone out . . . And, since to our adventurer, all that he thought, saw or imagined, corresponded to what he had read, he represented it to himself as a castle with its four towers and chapels of shining silver; nor did it lack raised drawbridge and deep moat—or any other of the features proper to such castles.'

If Don Quixote saw an inn and imagined a castle, the traveller in Spain today might well see a castle—and find it to be an inn. What the tourist, in search of a beer, more solid refreshment or a comfortable bed, had first taken to be an abandoned mediaeval keep, might indeed prove to be a Parador. . . .

There are upwards of thirty converted castles, monasteries and baronial houses scattered over Spain and forming part of a network of some eighty government-run hotels and restaurants, strategically placed in areas of the country where ordinary hotel facilities are not available. The purpose of the first few Paradores and Albergues de Carretera ('wayside inns') may have been to provide comfortable accommodation for motorists en route for the playgrounds of the Mediterranean or recognized tourist attractions like Granada or Seville; but, as the programme gathered impetus, it began to serve other and more far-reaching ends. On the one hand, it has made possible the preservation of numerous very significant historical sites which would otherwise have decayed; and on the other, it has allowed visitors to penetrate the real Spain: from the sandy coves of the Cantabrian coast, the green heights of the Picos de Europa, the myriad *rías* of Galicia, the windswept plateau of the two Castiles and the lush *huertas* of Valencia, to the dazzling lunar landscapes of Jerez de la Frontera and Cadiz.

It is human nature to take an interest in local history when on holiday; and from Stratford-on-Avon to Santiago de Compostela, the provision of guided tours and illustrated brochures has become a flourishing industry. The guide, accompanied by a shuffling flock which he regales with abundant dates and episodes from the lives of local heroes, has become a commonplace of the tourist scene. Such detailed information is difficult to absorb and quickly forgotten because the audience is often sublimely ignorant of the history of the country as a whole—the Emperor Charles V is as much of an unknown quantity as the Conde-Duque de Olivares. The ordinary guide book tends to suffer from the same disadvantage: a profusion of detail, unrewarding except in a broader historical context.

The arrangement of this book is therefore different. The Paradores have been located in time, rather than in place and on a regional basis—their geographical position may easily be checked on the sketch-maps in the text or the large map on the end-papers. The scheme is to set a historical period and then to illustrate it in more detail by a description of the events and persons connected with a particular Parador of historical interest.

Like all formal schemes, it suffers from ambiguity. Many of the Paradores were first built at one period, later to be reconstructed and to play a significant role at different epochs of Spanish history. Such, for example, is the castle of Fuenterrabía, first built by King Sancho Abarca of Navarre in the tenth century, extended by Sancho el Fuerte in the eleventh, and later associated with the Catholic Monarchs, the Emperor Charles V, Philip III, Philip IV and the French Kings Francis I and Louis XIV. Should a Parador be related to the date of its first construction, or to the events of a different period of perhaps greater historical interest, to which it is relevant because of its situation and former occupants? This latter is what we have preferred; and if our choice may sometimes seem arbitrary, an account of the building's earlier and later history is also supplied.

The Paradores can be used as the point of departure for a historical pilgrimage, either of Spain as a whole or of a particular region. They may also form a springboard for a very different exploration. The regions of Spain are strongly differentiated, and in nothing more than their regional cooking and wines. Andalusia is known for its fried dishes; the Extremadura for its hams; Old Castile, for its roast sucking pig and baby lamb; Valencia, for *paella* and rice; the north coast for its shellfish and varied methods of preparing it. So in wines, the country can offer a great deal more than sherry: one need only mention the classical growths of the Rioja, the robust Valdepeñas or the delicate and perfumed 'green wines' of Galicia, with their elusive sparkle.

Architectural and scenic beauties are best appreciated when the inner man is also satisfied; and in these strained and nerve-racking times a good meal with a pleasant bottle of wine remains one of the simplest and socially least damaging of enjoyments. When Richard Ford travelled Spain on horseback during the early 1830s he could describe it as a 'hungry, thirsty, tealess, beefless, beerless land'. This is certainly no longer the case; at the Paradores a representative selection of regional dishes and wines is available. The culinary notes which round off the descriptions of the Paradores will perhaps form a helpful footnote to regional food and wine. A selection of recipes is included for those who wish to try some of the dishes at home; between them, they form a résumé of the cooking of the country as a whole.

At the end of the book the reader will find a complete list of all the establishments belonging to the Ministry of Information and Tourism (M.I.T.), including Paradores (hotels), Albergues (inns), Refugios (winter sports centres) and Hosterías (restaurants). It goes without saying that the visitor will find a whole range of other hostelries, ranging from luxury hotels to country *fondas*, from which to explore this most diverse of countries; but the book centres on the historic Paradores. They are of all periods, and they mirror the history and creature comforts of Spain at large.

Below: The inn at Puerto Lápice mentioned in *Don Quixote*.

1 How the Paradores Began

The word 'Parador' has been derived from the Arabic *waradah*, a 'halting place', and is certainly related to the Spanish *parada*, used in the same sense. Like so much else in Spain, the origins of the modern luxury hotel would therefore seem to stretch back to the Moorish invasion of 711. Writing in 1846, Richard Ford emphasizes the oriental character of the *parador* of his day when he describes it as 'a huge caravansary for the reception of waggons, carts, and beasts of burden' and further recounts how the assembled company would settle around the kitchen fireplace with repeated invitations to share in their severally prepared meals.

To illustrate how radically arrangements for the reception of travellers have changed, something should be said about the type of accommodation available until well after the turn of the present century. As might be expected, the most sophisticated establishment, the *fonda*, was to be found only in large towns; it was the nearest to a hotel in that it took in only human beings, and not horses or mules, and furthermore served meals to its guests. The other urban establishment, the *posada*—so-called because it was a house of *repose* after the travels of the day—was primarily devoted to beasts of burden, and its keeper was obliged to provide only lodging, salt and facilities for his guests to cook what they had brought with them. For these services he charged a small sum for the *ruido de casa*—the noise or disturbance occasioned by the visitors and their mounts.

The country inns, *ventas*, *paradores* and *mesones*, were even more exclusively laid out for the entertainment of animals rather than men; and this related to the state of the roads in the Peninsula until comparatively modern times. The basic network had been established by the Romans and little was done to improve it until the time of the Spanish Bourbons in the eighteenth century, when Charles III in particular improved the main routes between Madrid and the larger provincial cities so as to make them suitable for regular coach traffic. It is said of the expensive improvements to the high road to La Coruña that the king asked if it had been paved with silver—a pun on the Spanish corruption of the old Roman *via lata* into *camino de plata*. At this same time, the condition of the famous *Vía de la Plata* from Mérida to Salamanca (from which the present Parador at Mérida takes its name) was typical of even the major subsidiary routes. Ford describes how the 'grey granite line' of the Roman causeway stretched 'across the aromatic wastes, like the vertebrae of an extinct mammoth. . . . Nature ever young and gay festoons the ruins with necklaces of flowers and creepers, and hides the rents and wrinkles of odious, all-dilapidating Time, or man's worse neglect, as a pretty maid decorates a shrivelled dowager's with diamonds', while 'the Spanish muleteer creeps along by its side in a track which he has made through the sand or pebbles . . .'

The ruinous state of the roads and their unsuitability for military operations played a major part in Napoleon's eventual defeat in the Peninsular War and also in Sir John Moore's disastrous retreat to La Coruña. So appalling were the tracks across the Portuguese frontier that he despatched most of his guns and cavalry by a great loop to the south and waited impotently in Salamanca, while Napoleon shattered the Spanish armies and entered Madrid.

It is therefore not surprising that the country inns provided above all for the welfare of the indispensable horse or mule. The *paradores* were even more exclusively adapted for the reception of livestock, since they differed from the *ventas* and *mesones* in being located on the outskirts of the towns, where the drovers and their flocks could avoid the heavy local duties levied at their gates.

In Ford's words, 'The country *Parador, Meson, Posada* and *Venta* call it how you will, is the Roman *stabulum*, whose original intention was the housing of cattle, while the accommodation of travellers was secondary, and so it is in Spain to this day. The accommodation for the *beast* is excellent; cool roomy stables, ample mangers, a never-failing supply of fodder and water, every comfort and luxury which the animal is capable of enjoying, is ready on the spot; as regards *man*, it is just the reverse; he must forage abroad for anything he may want. Only a small part of the barn is allotted to him, and then he is lodged among the brutes below, or among the trusses and sacks of their food in the lofts above. He finds, in spite of all this, that if he asks the owner what he has got, he will be told that "there is everything, *hay de todo*", just as the rogue of a *ventero* informed Sancho Panza, that his empty larder contained all the birds of the air, all the beasts of the earth, all the fishes of the sea—a Spanish magnificence of phrase, which, when reduced to plain English, too often means, as in that case, there is everything you have brought with you.'

An inn of the sort habitually frequented by Ford during his travels and also by his contemporary George Borrow, while peddling bibles on behalf of the British and Foreign Bible Society, still exists on the main road from Madrid to the south. With open courtyard and balconied sleeping quarters, it has been modernized and is

10

open to tourists, and is in fact situated at Puerto Lápice, the scene of Don Quixote's first adventure.

The reception to be expected by the nineteenth-century traveller is again vividly described by Ford. 'All the operations of cookery and eating, of killing and sousing in boiling water, plucking, etcetera, all preparatory as well as final, go on in the open kitchen. They are carried out by the *ventera* and her daughters or maids, or by some crabbed, smoke-dried, shrivelled old she-cat, that is, or at least is called, the *tia*, my 'aunt' and who is the subject of the good-humoured remarks of the courteous and hungry traveller before dinner, and of his full stomach jests afterwards. The assembled parties crowd round the fire, watching and assisting each other at their own savoury messes, "*Un ojo a la sarten y otro a la gata*"—one eye to the pan, the other to the real cat, whose very existence in a *venta*, and among the pots, is a miracle.'

After dinner the peasants lay down with their beasts, while the better-heeled ascended to the gallery, where 'An eager welcome awaits the traveller at bedtime; his arrival is a godsend to the creeping tribe, who, like the *ventero*, have no regular larder; it is not upstairs that he eats, but where *he* is eaten.' Complaints were useless. Borrow recalls how he and his valet, after being shown to 'a tolerably decent chamber', were rudely turned out on the arrival of a waggon filled with travellers from Madrid as 'two vagabonds whom nobody knew', while Ford remarks that if, for example, 'you tell the landlord that his wine is more sour than his vinegar, he will gravely reply, "Señor, that cannot be, for both came out of the same cask".'

The great foreign travellers of the day were the English; and it was partly English influence which led to the reformation of the Spanish inn. On the one hand the British financing of railways resulted in a demand for a better type of accommodation; and on the other, refugees from the Carlist Wars of the 1830s and 1870s, many of whom migrated to London, returned to Spain with accounts of foreign innovations: 'Then and there suspicion crossed their minds, although they seldom will admit it, that Spain was not altogether the richest, strongest, and first of nations, but that she might take a hint or two in a few trifles, among which perhaps accommodations for man and beast might be included . . .

'Rooms are to be papered, brick floors to be exchanged for boards, carpets to be laid down, fireplaces to be made, and bells are to be hung, incredible as it may appear to all who remember Spain as it was. They will ring the knell of nationhood; and we shall be much mistaken if the grim old Cid, when the first one is pulled at Burgos, does not answer it for himself by knocking the innovator down. Nay, more, for wonders never cease; vague rumours are abroad that secret and solitary closets are contemplated, in which, by some magical mechanism, sudden waters are to gush forth . . .'

Prescient as Ford was, he could hardly foresee the eventual development of the modern Parador; and the 'grim old Cid' might well find himself quite at home in the baronial halls of a Benavente or Fuenterrabía. The bell that tolled in the twentieth century was in fact for the romantic and monied traveller of the eighteenth and the nineteenth, for whom the hardships of his journey were part and parcel of a voyage of discovery. Foreign travel expands in step with the availability of safe and rapid transport; and what gave it impetus was first the development of the railways, and later of the car and airplane.

At the same time, the twentieth century saw a profound change in social conditions. The millions who flooded into large cities to work in offices or on a production line and spent the larger part of their existence in artificially-conditioned surroundings displayed a yearning for the open spaces, fresh air and sunshine—whether on a Mediterranean beach, camping or in the mountains. And the nineteenth-century tradition was not entirely lost: visits to the Alhambra and Santiago de Compostela represent the sale of memories and emotions evoked by a past, which, seen from a comfortable distance, seems picturesque and less greyly monotonous than the everyday routine. A general rise in the standard of living and paid holidays resulted in a tourist explosion, of which a Spanish writer, Luis Fernandez Fuster, has said: 'It spread like a contagious disease; it was like the swirl of leaves from a row of trees shaken by a gust of wind.'

The governments of the less industrialized countries, like Italy, Spain, Portugal and Greece, were the first to grasp the economic possibilities of this restless desire for change of scene. In 1948— before the era of the package tour—175,892 foreign tourists visited Spain and spent some 100 million pesetas. By 1954, when mass tourism was only beginning, the figure had risen to almost 2 million, and foreign visitors left 730 million pesetas in the country—in comparison with the 228 million earned by the export of citrus fruit, which had previously been Spain's largest single source of foreign currency.

Over the centuries Spain had traditionally remained remote and aloof beyond the barrier of the Pyrenees—apart from the sunshine, it was perhaps this feeling of the exotic which first attracted visitors from abroad; and the first official attempt to encourage foreign tourism was the creation by Royal Decree of a *Comisón Nacional* in 1905, charged with propaganda and the improvement of rail services and hotel facilities. It was replaced in 1911 by the *Comisaría Regia del Turismo*, composed of representatives from various

12

interested Ministries. It was this body, inspired by the Marqués de la Vega Inclán—who may be regarded as the architect of organized tourism in Spain—that planned the first Parador in 1926.

In some ways the Parador programme represents a reversion to the romantic ideas of the early nineteenth-century travellers. It is with something of the same spirit of adventure that one now sets out in a car for the most inaccessible regions of the country, knowing that, wherever one heads, there will be, if not a *venta*, a Parador within driving distance. Be that as it may, the first Parador was planned to open up the rolling mountains and pine forests of the Sierra de Gredos west of Madrid to the tourist with a taste for the remote and an eye for natural beauty. The mountains were, and still are, the haunt of the *Capra hispánica*, a species of wild goat hunted by King Alfonso XIII (and General Franco after him); and it was King Alfonso who personally chose the site on a ridge south of Avila.

The Parador of Gredos was an immediate attraction; and in 1928 the *Patronato Nacional de Turismo*, which succeeded the Royal Commission, set up a *Junta de Paradores y Hosterías del Reino* with instructions to plan further Paradores in regions not adequately served by existing hotels. This impressively aristocratic body—it numbered no less than three marchionesses, four counts and a baroness—went to work with a will. The first fruit of its plans was the Hotel Atlántico opened in Cadiz in 1929, as being strategically situated at a point where the shipping routes from America converged on the Mediterranean. It remains the only hotel in the present network; and the Junta very early addressed itself to the conversion of abandoned castles, monasteries and palaces, which would otherwise have fallen into ruins. The first to be inaugurated were the Castles of Oropesa and Ciudad Rodrigo (1930 and 1931), the former Palace of the Ortegas at Ubeda (1931) and an Hostería (restaurant) installed in the Colegio Trilingüe of the ancient University of Alcalá de Henares (1930)—all described in detail in the following section.

In addition to Paradores and Hosterías, the Junta made provision for a number of less elaborate establishments: the Albergues de Carretera. These were sited along main routes for the convenience of motorists, and in isolated spots where it had previously been impossible to obtain a comfortable room, bath and adequate restaurant facilities.

Anyone familiar with the state of the Spanish roads as late as the early 1950s will realise how sensibly the Junta planned. In an age when motorways are becoming as common—and as crowded—in Spain as elsewhere, the narrow poplar-lined *carreteras*, cratered with pot-holes, swerving abruptly through a farmyard with a flurry

13

of hens, and provided with a gaunt, unsheltered petrol pump every fifty kilometers or so, seem as remote as the bridle-paths travelled by Borrow and Ford. Nevertheless, on roads like these, with the further obstacles of farm carts crawling out at dawn and dusk, or the Andalusian peasant sprawling in *siesta* at the point where the heat and the wine overcame him, 200 kilometres were a respectable day's journey. The Junta accordingly sited the Albergue de Manzanares 176km along the main road from Madrid to the south and the next 124km further on at Bailen, where the road forks for Cadiz or Granada.

It was estimated that on average the Albergues would be visited by three cars a day; and on the basis of four passengers to a car, accommodation was limited to four double rooms and four singles, together with a lounge and restaurant seating thirty. For reasons of economy and so that the Albergues were easily identifiable, design was standardized—the most striking feature being the bow-fronted restaurant with french windows opening on to a terrace. The stay, as it still is, was limited to 48 hours. Because of the vastly increased traffic today, a number of the Albergues are now being phased out and replaced by modern Paradores with more facilities and much larger numbers of rooms. Some of the Albergues, like that at Antequera, are remarkable for a high standard of cuisine; and Manzanares, once a staging post on the old road to Cadiz, is now a popular rendezvous for Sunday lunchers from Madrid.

The Republican government which came into power in April 1931 carried on with these plans; and when the Civil War broke out in 1936 there were five Paradores in operation, in addition to the Hotel Atlántico in Cadiz, seven Albergues and the Hostería at Alcalá. During the war operations were, of course, suspended, some of the buildings being used as hospitals and others, like the Hostería of Alcalá de Heneres being severely damaged—it has happily been rebuilt with loving care for the original detail.

During the Franquist era the conversion of historic buildings and the construction of entirely new establishments proceeded at a greatly accelerated pace, as is best illustrated by the chronological list in the next section. Although new buildings predominated and the scheme was extended to *Refugios*, constructed in mountain areas as centres for winter sports, many of the new Paradores were built on sites of historical interest. One such example is the extremely comfortable and well-equipped La Aruzafa on the outskirts of Córdoba, which takes its name from al-Rusafa, the summer residence of the first Emir of Córdoba, 'Abd-al-Rahman I—itself a nostalgic recreation of the summer palace erected by his ancestor, the caliph Hisham, among gardens irrigated by the

14

Euphrates. The modern Parador is a convenient base for exploring both Córdoba and the adjacent ruins of an even more splendid Moorish palace, the legendary Madinat al-Zahra' of 'Abd-al-Rahman III.

There now exist 64 Paradores, 17 Albergues, 5 Hosterías, 3 Refugios and 1 hotel, but the exact number actually open varies, as older establishments are from time to time closed for repair and renovation. Over the period 1928–1972 the accommodation had risen from 30 beds and 80 restaurant seats to 3,862 beds and places for 7,044 in the dining rooms. A further set of figures illustrates the scale of the enterprise: during 1974–75 the Paradores and other establishments entertained 500,000 guests, of whom 250,000 were Spanish; 100,000 North American; 78,000 English and English-speaking; 78,000 French; and 55,000 German.

In the early years the buildings reconstructed as Paradores were handed over to private management, as are the *Pousadas* in Portugal today; but the government soon assumed complete responsibility for running them.

By 1951 tourism was playing such an important role in the Spanish economy that the Ministerio de Información y Turismo (M.I.T.) was created to supervise and further it; and in 1958 control of what was now a national network of state-run establishments was delegated to an autonomous organization within the Ministry, the Administración Turistica Española. While this body is responsible for a variety of central services, including works, ware-housing, accounts, and publicity, individual Paradores are run like privately-owned hotels. Like other hotels in Spain, their prices are fixed in conformity with the official classification of their facilities: in fact, out of a possible five stars, the Paradores rate either four or three, and the Albergues from four to two. Although the purpose of the network has never been to make large profits—any surplus is more than swallowed up in further development—the establishments are expected to be self-supporting. Any surplus is transferred to a central account, from which the deficit of less profitable establishments is met.

The managers, known as Administrators, are experienced hoteliers and are chosen by competitive examination, after which they undergo a trial period in different establishments. They are then allowed considerable liberty. Unlike the units of so many hotel chains, no one Parador is quite the same in style as another. It is true that one can always rely on a comfortable, and often more than spacious, bedroom with private bathroom and air-conditioning when necessary; the lounges are large, imaginatively decorated in keeping with the period of the building, and often equipped with a small library of books relating to the region; and the tables in

15

2 Paradores, Albergues, Refugios and Hosterías in order of their opening to the public

(The names following the Paradores refer to Provinces, not towns.)

1.	Parador of Gredos, Avila	1928	
2.	Hotel Atlántico, Cadiz	1930	
3.	Parador of Oropesa, Toledo	1930	
4.	Hostería of Alcalá de Henares, Madrid	1930	
5.	Parador of Ciudad Rodrigo, Salamanca	1931	
6.	Parador of Ubeda, Jaén	1931	
7.	Albergue of Manzanares, Ciudad Real	1932	
8.	Albergue of Bailen, Jaén	1932	(now Parador)
9.	Albergue of Benicarló, Castellón	1933	(now Parador)
10.	Parador of Mérida, Badajoz	1933	
11.	Albergue of Quintanar, Toledo	1933	(catering school 1966, closed 1970)
12.	Albergue of Aranda de Duero, Burgos	1935	
13.	Albergue of La Bañeza, León	1935	
14.	Albergue of Medinaceli, Soria	1935	(Hostería 1970, closed 1972)
15.	Albergue of Antequera, Málaga	1940	
16.	Refugio of Aliva, Santander	1944	(closed 1974)
17.	Parador of Andújar, Jaén	1944	(closed for repairs 1970)
18.	Parador of Granada, Granada	1945	
19.	Albergue of Puebla de Sanabria, Zamora	1945	
20.	Parador of Santillana, Santander	1946	
21.	Albergue of Puerto Lumbreras, Murcia	1946	
22.	Hostería of Gibralfaro, Málaga	1948	(Parador 1965)
23.	Parador of Cruz de Tejada, Canaries	1949	
24.	Parador of Arrecife, Canaries	1951	(closed for repairs 1970)
25.	Parador of Riaño, León	1951	(closed for repairs 1969)
26.	Parador of Santa Cruz de la Palma, Canaries	1951	
27.	Refugio of Ordesa, Huesca	1953	(closed for repairs 1969)
28.	Parador of Pajares, Oviedo	1953	

29.	Parador of Pontevedra, Pontevedra	1954	
30.	Parador del Golf, Málaga	1956	
31.	Parador of Teruel, Teruel	1956	
32.	Albergue of Tordesillas, Valladolid	1958	
33.	Albergue of Ribadeo, Lugo	1958	(Parador 1972)
34.	Parador of El Ferrol, La Coruña	1959	
35.	Albergue of Villafranca del Bierzo, León	1959	
36.	Parador of Las Cañadas Teide, Canaries	1960	
37.	Parador of Córdoba, Córdoba	1960	
38.	Albergue of Villacastín, Segovia	1961	
39.	Parador of Madrigal de las Altas Torres, Avila	1964	(closed 1973)

1965

40. Refugio of Juanar, Málaga
41. Burgo de las Naciones, Madrid (summer Albergue since 1966)
42. Albergue of Ribadelago, Zamora (closed 1972)
43. Albergue of Santa María de Huerta, Soria
44. Parador of Nerja, Málaga
45. Parador of Santo Domingo de la Calzada, Logrono
46. Parador of Guadalupe, Cáceres
47. Parador of Jaén, Jaén (closed for reconstruction)
48. Parador of Cazorla, Jaén
49. Parador of Jávea, Alicante

1966

50. Parador of Ayamonte, Huelva
51. Parador of Aiguablava, Gerona
52. Parador of Mojacar, Almeria
53. Parador of Alarcón, Cuenca
54. Parador of Jarandilla de la Vera, Cáceres
55. Parador of Puertomarin, Lugo
56. Parador of Cambados, Pontevedra
57. Parador of Avila, Avila
58. Parador of Valle del Arán, Lérida
59. Parador of Fuente Dé, Santander
60. Parador of Bayona, Pontevedra
61. Parador of Olite, Navarra
62. Parador of El Saler, Valencia
63. Parador of Arcos de la Frontera, Cadiz
64. Parador of Sierra Nevada, Granada
65. Parador of Soria, Soria

1967

66. Parador of Verín, Orense
67. Albergue of Fuentes de Oñoro (closed)
68. Hostería of Arties, Lérida
69. Parador of Gijón, Asturias
70. Parador of Villalba, Lugo
71. Hostería of Pedraza de la Sierra, Segovia

1968

72. Parador of Musques (closed in 1972)
73. Hostería of Alcañíz, Teruel (Parador 1970)
74. Parador of Lequeitio, Vizcaya (closed 1972)
75. Parador of Tuy, Pontevedra
76. Parador of Zamora, Zamora
77. Parador of Toledo, Toledo
78. Parador of Fuenterrabía, Guipúzcoa
79. Parador of El Aaiun, Spanish Sahara (no longer in Spanish territory)
80. Parador of Fuertaventura, Canaries
81. Parador of Zafra, Badajoz
82. Parador of Mazagón, Huelva
83. Parador of Bielsa, Huesca

1970

84. Albergue of Albacete, Albacete

1972

85. Hostería of Cáceres, Cáceres
86. Hostería of Madrid (closed 1973)
87. Parador of Benavente, Zamora
88. Parador of Vich, Barcelona
89. Parador of Gomera, Canaries
90. Parador of Melilla, Spanish Morocco

1976

91. Parador of Calahorra, Logrono
92. Parador of Cervera de Pisuerga, Palencia
93. Parador of Monzón de Campos, Palencia
94. Parador of Cardona, Barcelona
95. Parador of Sos de Rey Católico, Zaragoza
96. Parador of Sigüenza, Guadalajara

Further Paradores are under construction or are planned at:
Carmona, Sevilla
Santa Cruz de Tenerife, Canaries
Almagro, Ciudad Real
Elorrio, Vizcaya
Argomaniz, Alava
Chinchón, Madrid
Tortosa, Tarragona
Siguenza, Guadalajara
Trujillo, Cáceres

3 The Historic Paradores: their cooking and wines

Prehistory and the study of the nameless tribes which inhabited Europe during the Ice Age is not the most inviting of subjects. It is difficult to relate their activities to the subsequent history of Spain or other countries; although it may be of interest that, with the recession of the polar ice-cap, the British Isles were first populated and civilized from southern Spain. Nevertheless, the vivid and striking cave drawings made during the Upper Palaeolithic era some 15,000 years ago, such as those at Altamira in northern Spain, must fire any imagination.

The Cantabrian coast, bordering the Atlantic, and the mountain range of the Picos de Europa, whose foothills, carpeted with beech, rise steeply from it, remained a stronghold of the indigenous tribes during the invasions of modern times. The Iberians of Cantabria fiercely resisted the Romans; and the region, which was never penetrated by the Moors, became a bastion of the Christian Reconquest. Among the theories put forward to account for the tenacious independence and strange language of the present-day Basques is one that they are the direct descendants of the primitive Iberians.

Gil Blas: Santillana del Mar

The Parador of Gil Blas near Santander is next door to the Caves of Altamira, discovered by S. de Sautuola in 1875. The paintings, though smaller than those later discovered at Lascaux in the Dordogne in 1940, remain among the most striking that are known; and the confined rock chamber, approached by a narrow, sloping passage, has been called the Sistine Chapel of Palaeolithic Art. Some 150 in number, they represent bison, deer, boars and horses and are painted in red and yellow ochre with a black outline. Many of the most impressive are on the ceiling (the largest is 2 metres long), so that one must lie on one's back to gain the best impression; and the artists have made skilful use of the natural contours of the rock to obtain a degree of relief. The cave at Altamira (currently closed for restoration) is not the only one in the region: there are others at Puente Víesgo and Ramales de la Victoria, rich both in drawings and other prehistoric remains.

The Parador is named after the hero of Lesage's picaresque romance *Gil Blas de Santillane*. Completed in 1735, the book is set in Spain, but its characters, like the preposterous quack, Dr. Sangrado, reflect contemporary life in Paris.

The little town of Santillana, now a National Monument, sprang up around a monastery built to preserve the remains of Saint Juliana, martyred in Asia Minor, and received its first charter from Ferdinand I of Castile, who campaigned deep into Moorish territory

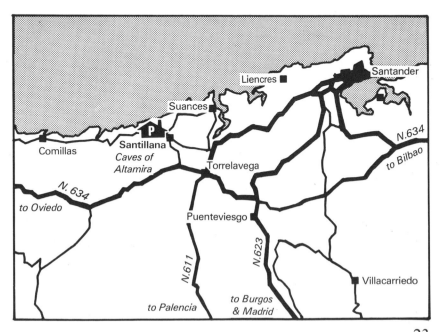

after the break up of the Córdoban caliphate (see page 72) during the first decades of the eleventh century. The most remarkable building in Santillana today is the Romanesque Colegiata, built in the twelfth century on the site of the former monastery. Besides the tomb of Saint Juliana, it contains a splendid twelfth-century cloister, numerous Romanesque capitals carved with flowers, animals and human figures, and a beautiful Gothic altar-piece with glowing paintings ascribed to Jorge Inglés, 1453.

The town itself, with its cobbled streets, balconies vivid with flowers and old-fashioned open-air washing place, has been called the birthplace of the Cantabrian aristocracy. The baronial houses, with richly-carved stone escutcheons, stand side by side. The earliest date from the thirteenth century, but they are predominantly Baroque and belonged to families like the Tagle, Estrada, Cossio and Peredo. One of the town's most famous sons was the Marquis of Santillana, the celebrated fifteenth-century poet; and the aristocratic tradition continues. The former palace of the Abades now belongs to the Archduchess Margarita of Austria.

The Parador is installed in the seventeenth-century palace of the Bareda Bracho family, of which the original character has been carefully preserved. Apart from its accessibility to the Caves of Altamira, it is a convenient base for visits to the sandy beaches of the Cantabrian coast and excursions to the Picos de Europa, with their rare mountain flowers and swift-flowing trout and salmon streams.

Above: The dining room at the Parador of Gil Blas, Santillana del Mar.

Gastronomically, Cantabria is best-known for its shellfish from the cool waters and rocky shores of the Atlantic. These include lobsters (*bogavantes*); prawns (*gambas*), served either cold, grilled (*a la plancha*) or in a spicy sauce with garlic and chillis (*al pil pil*); shrimps (*camarones*); cockles (*chirlas*); and mussels (*almejas*), delicious when eaten cold as an aperitif in a sauce made with olive oil, parsley and garlic. *Percebes*, a succulent species of edible barnacle, resembling nothing so much as a clump of lobster's claws, are also delicious as an aperitif. Another delicacy is the large spider crab (*centollo*), prepared by cooking the meat in white wine and replacing it in the shell. The port area of adjacent Santander is called the Sardinero; and the coast is famous for the quality of its sardines, a great favourite with summer visitors when fresh fried or cooked over a charcoal grill in the beach restaurants.

There is also abundant salmon, trout and game from the mountains lying back from the coast. Among its specialities, the Parador of Gil Blas lists *Pucherete Gil Blas*, a rich vegetable soup containing the spiced *chorizo* sausage; *Cocido Montañés*, a variant of those rib-warming stews made with a basis of chick peas, for which Old Castile is famous; and custard made with fresh cream from the mountain pastures.

A modern Parador in the adjacent region of Asturias, the Molino Viejo in Gijón, offers an even wider choice of regional dishes: *Sopa de*

24

Avellanas is a soup made with pounded hazelnuts and served with croûtons; *Tortilla asturiana* is a most individual version of the Spanish omelette, containing minced meat, tomatoes, peppers and cheese; *Fabada asturiana*, the classical dish of the Asturias, is a nourishing peasant stew, here prepared with great sophistication from butter beans, blood sausage, *chorizo*, bacon and shoulder of pork. Fish dishes include *Calderete de pescado*, akin to *Bouillabaisse*, and *Merluza a la sidra*, hake served in a rich sauce made from brandy, mussels, cider, flour, boiled eggs and red peppers. Asturias is a region of sauces; and pork, veal and ham are roasted and appropriately embellished. Among the sweets, perhaps the most individual is *Arroz requemada asturiana*, a milky rice pudding, flavoured with aniseed, cinnamon and lemon and coated with brittle caramel. Neither the Provinces of Santander nor Asturias make any wine of note; but their cider is the best in Spain.

FABADA ASTURIANA
Serves 4
1lb 2oz (500gm) *Fabes* (a variety of butter beans)
7oz (200gm) *chorizo*
7oz (200gm) *morcilla* (or blood sausage)
2oz (60gm) *jamón serrano* (or cooked ham)
4oz (110gm) *tocino* (or belly of pork)
4oz (110gm) *lacón* (ham bone)
Saffron
Salt and pepper

Right: Baronial houses in Santillana del Mar. Overleaf left: Palaeolithic cave drawings from Altamira. Overleaf right: Open air washing place in Santillana del Mar.

25

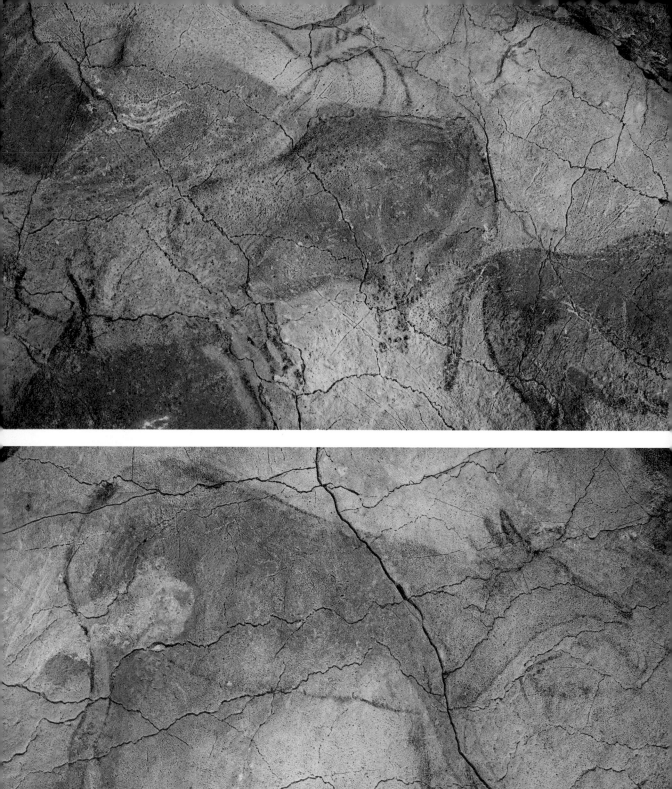

Above: The Torre del Príncipe in the grounds of the Parador of the Conde de Gondomar, probably built by the tenth century and now used as a lighthouse. Left: View from the grounds of the Parador of the Conde de Gondomar.

Put all the ingredients except the saffron, salt and pepper into a stew pot. Cover with cold water, bring to the boil, then reduce the flame and simmer very gently for 1½ hours or until the butter beans are tender. Check the seasoning before serving.

GAMBAS AL AJILLO
PRAWNS WITH HOT CHILLIS
Serves 2
Olive oil
½lb (225gm) prawns, peeled and cooked
3 cloves of garlic, peeled and finely chopped
2 chillis
Cover the bottoms of a couple of *cazuelas* or small casseroles with a little olive oil, add half of the garlic to each and fry slowly. Add a chilli to each *cazuela* and then the prawns. When they begin to cook, fry for 5 minutes. Place the *cazuelas* on plates and serve piping hot from the fire.

SOPA DE AVELLANAS
HAZELNUT SOUP
Serves 4
2oz (60gm) toasted breadcrumbs
1½ pints (9dl) chicken stock (if necessary, made from a cube)
Pinch of saffron
1 clove of garlic, peeled
2oz (60gm) hazelnuts
Salt and pepper
Pour the chicken stock into a saucepan, add the breadcrumbs and stir into a smooth paste. Grind the saffron, garlic and nuts in a mortar, then stir into the pan. Season with salt and pepper and simmer slowly for 10 minutes.

TORTILLA ASTURIANA
ASTURIAN OMELETTE
Serves 2
Olive oil
1oz (30gm) minced veal or other cooked meat
1 shallot or small onion, finely chopped
2 tomatoes, blanched and cut up
1 canned pepper, cut up
1oz (30gm) grated cheese
Salt and pepper
4 eggs
Heat a little oil in a pan and fry the meat slowly with the onion for about 10 minutes. Drain off the oil for further use. Add the tomatoes and pimiento and cook slowly for 5 minutes. Meanwhile beat the eggs in a bowl, then add the contents of the pan, the cheese, and a little salt and pepper.
Put a little oil into the pan, return it to the fire, and when the oil begins to smoke, add the egg mixture and cook for a minute or two until browned on the bottom. Place a plate on top and reverse. Without adding further oil to the pan, slide back the omelette to brown the uncooked side. Serve with all speed.

Until the arrival of the Romans the indigenous tribes which inhabited the Iberian Peninsula could in no sense be called a nation. There had been earlier foreign visitations from the Phoenicians; and the Greeks, who are said to have introduced the vine and the olive, formed trading posts on the Mediterranean coast, but without attempting to move far inland. The Carthaginians made more determined inroads, especially in the south; after the first Punic War, which ended in 242 BC, the Carthaginian Hamilcar Barca attempted to use the Peninsula as a base for an eventual attack on Italy. This culminated in his son Hannibal's great expedition in 219 BC, which brought the Romans to the area in counter-attack.

The Carthaginians finally abandoned the Peninsula in 206 BC, after being defeated several times by Publius Cornelius Scipio. The Romans then moved into the region in strength and turned their attention to the subjugation of the native population, whom Roman historians termed 'Celtiberians' and represented as a brave and relentless enemy, prodiga gens animae. *In fact they gave Rome more trouble than any other race within the Empire; and it was from them that the legionaries are said to have borrowed their short swords and heavy spears.*

In general the local tribes were too small and disorganized to offer large-scale resistance; but it required the despatch of a strong army under the elder Cato during the last decade of the second century BC, and energetic action by Julius Caesar, to bring the country to heel. It was only under Augustus Caesar (63 BC–14 AD) that the country was finally pacified.

Conde de Gondomar: Bayona

The Parador of the Conde de Gondomar at Bayona has a special association with the turbulent period of the Roman conquest. It is situated on the Peninsula of Monte Real (of which the Count of Gondomar was a former governor), jutting into the Vigo *Ría* (or estuary) some way south of the city. It is a peerless site, surrounded by water, with a backdrop of constantly shifting clouds—a haunted shore, crowded by the ghosts of history.

The place was surrounded by a fortified wall long before it was colonized by the Romans; and it was here that Viriatus, a tribal chieftain, staged a revolt in 140 BC and defeated the troops sent against him by Servilianus. A century later, Julius Caesar himself lost a battle against rebels who had taken refuge in the Cíes Islands offshore. Less brutal than Cato, he recognized their bravery by giving them honourable terms when hunger compelled their surrender.

But this was only the beginning of Bayona's long history. After the decline of the Roman Empire and the invasion of the country by waves of 'barbarians' from the north, Monte Real was captured by King Reccared, the first of the Visigoths to be converted to Catholicism, in 586. After the Muslim invasion from Africa in 711, it was held by the Moors for twenty years before being recaptured in 750 by Alfonso I of Asturias, the 'Catholic', during the first of the Christian counter-offensives. In 997, when the dying Caliphate of Córdoba staged one of its last great raids on the Christian north on the shrine of Santiago de Compostela, Monte Real fell briefly into the hands of al-Mansur the 'Victorious'. During the Middle Ages it was a stronghold of Henry of Trastámara in his fratricidal struggle with Pedro the Cruel of Castile; and it was from its massive battlements that in 1493 its inhabitants caught a glimpse of the '*Pinta*', one of Columbus's three caravels, on its way to the discovery of the New World. In 1585 it was courageously defended against an attack by Sir Francis Drake and his fleet; and the iron cannon, still trained on the blue expanse of Vigo Bay, bear silent witness to one of the last incidents in Bayona's warlike past, when it was used as a pirate haven for attacks on British and Dutch merchantmen during the eighteenth century.

The whole forty-five-acre peninsula, now occupied by gardens and planted with pine trees, oranges and lemons, forms the grounds of the Parador. It is ringed by a castellated wall three kilometres in length, along whose broad top it is possible to make a complete circuit of the domain. The gateways and other buildings are of various periods. The carving on an ancient well, feeding a cistern

Overleaf: The modern facade of the Parador of the Conde de Gondomar at Bayona.

31

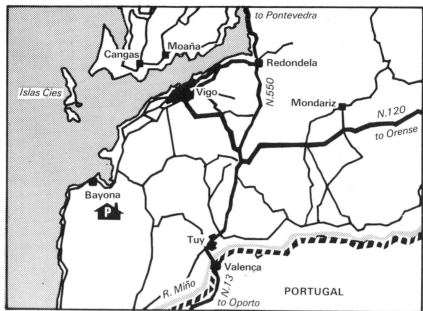

constructed by Philip IV in the seventeenth century is Roman; the Torre del Principe ('Prince's Tower'), now used as a lighthouse, probably existed before the Norman invasion of the region in the tenth century and was reconstructed by King Alfonso XI of Castile in the fourteenth. Near the main entrance one can still see the 'Casa de Pedro Madruga', named after a semi-legendary soldier, who captured Monte Real in the name of Afonso V of Portugal in 1474. Of the arched gateways, the oldest, the Puerta del Sol, dating from the early sixteenth century, stood by an ancient highway paved with huge slabs of pre-Roman origin; and the seventeenth-century gate by which one now enters the precinct is surmounted by the Hapsburg double eagle of Philip IV.

The Parador is a large modern building, accommodating 165 guests and built in the style of a traditional Galician *Pazo* (or baronial dwelling) on the site of a palace, formerly a Franciscan friary, of the Marqués de Elduayen, from whose heirs M.I.T. bought the property in 1963. Features of the Parador are the valuable Renaissance furniture, antique clocks and hangings, and an extensive collection of old prints and watercolours by contemporary Galician artists. The grounds contain a private chapel, swimming pool and tennis courts. There is access to a yacht basin through a water-gate in the wall, and a golf course is being laid out near-by, so that the whole complex, with its extensive private grounds, is in the nature of a luxurious country club.

33

The approach to Bayona from the north, by way of Vigo and its *Ría*, affords a foretaste of its culinary specialities. The upper reaches of the wide and startlingly blue estuary, with the green mountains beyond, are dotted with what at first seem to be small black houseboats. They are in fact *Mejilloneras*—mobile platforms for fishing cultured mussels. And as one enters the grounds of the Parador, winding up the long drive between glowing banks of geraniums and groves of pines, one soon passes an impressive marisquería (shellfish bar).

The Parador serves most of the shellfish described in connection with the Cantabrian coast (see page 24) and prides itself on offering the widest possible choice. In addition to the varieties already mentioned, its regional menu lists: *langoustines*, scampi, *crevettes*, scallops and *nécoras* (a species of spider crab), as well as that typical Spanish favourite *Calamares en su tinta* (squid in its ink), a choice of whitefish and a *Zarzuela de pescados Rías Baixas*. Zarzuela is the Spanish word for a variety show; and a variety of fish in a piquant tomato sauce is just what this dish is. Of Catalan origin, it lends itself well to the splendid abundance of fresh fish from Galician waters.

As befits a luxury hotel, the Parador has a long list of the classic Spanish wines from the Rioja; but the natural accompaniment to Galician shellfish is one of the dry, flowery and slightly sparking *vinos verdes* ('green' or young wines) from the region, described in further detail in connection with the Parador de la Casa del Barón at Pontevedra (see page 193). Although you will have to go into the little

Opposite: A gateway in the grounds of the Parador of the Conde de Gondomar. The Hapsburg double eagle of the shield is that of Philip IV (1605–65). Left: The yacht basin from the grounds of the Parador of the Conde de Gondomar.

34

port of Bayona to obtain it—a pleasant enough way of stretching one's legs outside the grounds—the immediate locality produces a good vino tinto de Salnés, made from the Espadeiro grape typical of the neighbourhood. It is a red wine, dry to a degree, and the first mouthful is a shock; but it goes well enough with some of the stronger Galician dishes like *Callos a la gallega* (Galician tripe) or *Churrasco* (charcoal-grilled meat). Drink it stone-cold.

VIEIRAS DE LAS RIAS BAIXAS
BAKED SCALLOPS IN SHELL
Serves 2
4 scallops
A little chopped parsley
2 cloves of garlic, ground
1 shallot or 2 spring onions, finely chopped
Pinch of freshly ground black pepper
1 clove, ground
Pinch of freshly ground nutmeg
1 tablespoon of refined olive oil
Salt
Toasted breadcrumbs
Remove the scallops from their shells or get the fishmonger to do this for you—but keep and wash the shells for serving. Wash and dry the fish, then tumble them on a plate with all the ingredients except the olive oil and breadcrumbs. Now replace the scallops in their shells and sprinkle them with a little olive oil and breadcrumbs. Bake in a moderately hot oven (400°F, or Mark 6) for 15 minutes.

CALDERETA DE PESCADO
FISH STEW
Serves 4
The dish takes its name from the *caldereta* or stew pan used for cooking it.
Olive oil
2lb (1kg) assorted firm fish
4 large prawns
8 mussels
1 onion, finely chopped
1 teaspoon sweet paprika
Salt and pepper
1 dessertspoon chopped parsley
2fl oz (60ml) dry sherry
Pinch of nutmeg
1 canned red pepper, puréed
1 chilli
Heat some olive oil in a large earthenware *cazuela* or a stew pan. Cut the larger fish into smaller pieces, then add all the whitefish, turning it in the hot oil. Add the prawns, mussels, onion, sweet paprika, salt and pepper, together with a breakfast cup of water. Cook slowly over a low flame, taking care that the fish does not disintegrate. Stir in the parsley, sherry, nutmeg, pimiento and chilli, shaking the pan so that the contents do not stick. If the fish are large, allow 20 minutes slow cooking, or 15 minutes if they are small.

Opposite: Vigo Bay from the grounds of the Parador of the Conde de Gondomar.

POTE GALLEGO
GALICIAN HOT POT
Serves 4
1lb (450gm) butter beans
Small ham bone
4oz (110gm) tocino or belly of pork
8oz (225gm) spring cabbage
3 potatoes, peeled and cut up
1oz (30gm) pork fat
1 clove of garlic
Salt and pepper

View of Bayona from the grounds of the Parador of the Conde de Gondomar.

Soak the butter beans in cold water the previous night and leave the ham bone in water for a few hours also. Transfer the beans to a stew pan and cover with fresh water, add the ham bone and belly of pork and boil for 2 hours before adding the cabbage and potato.

Heat the pork fat in a frying pan, brown the garlic and then stir in a little of the stock from the stew pan. Transfer to the stew pan, season with salt and pepper, and continue simmering until the beans are tender. They may require up to 3 hours cooking in all.

Romanization of Hispania, as the new province was called, proceeded during the reign of Augustus and the first two and a half centuries AD. For the first time the country became a nation. Peace and a settled regime led to the development of agriculture; cities were built, each in the image of a little Rome, and were connected by a network of properly engineered roads. An extensive trade was established with other parts of the Empire, and the Roman legal system was introduced. The Emperors Trajan and Hadrian, the orator Quintilian and the agriculturalist Columella were all Spanish-born; Spanish legionaries fought as far afield as Britain. The Spanish language is today closer to Latin than modern Italian; and in its declining years the Empire left Spain the great legacy of Christianity.

Vía de la Plata: Mérida

In all of Spain, the Parador de La Vía de la Plata in Mérida near the Portuguese border, on the main road from Madrid to Lisbon, is the best place to study 'the grandeur that was Rome'. It was founded as *Augusta Emerita* by Augustus Caesar in 25 BC as the headquarters of his Ninth Legion and became the capital of the Province of Lusitania, corresponding roughly to present-day Portugal and the Spanish Extremadura. Writing in the fourth century, the poet Ausonius describes it as the ninth city of the Empire, taking precedence over Athens.

In and around Mérida today, its monuments, preserved in the dry air and baking heat of the Extremadura, are visible proof of its former glories and thriving populace; even now it is hardly possible to excavate the foundations for a new building without coming on a Roman pavement or the vestiges of a villa. The approach from Badajoz is by way of a bridge of sixty granite arches, probably built in 95 BC before the founding of the city. To the other side are a lofty aqueduct and the remains of a huge circus, including the chambers for the gladiators and the wild beasts, discovered in 1921. Even more impressive are the great amphitheatre, built of massive

Opposite: An interior patio of the Parador of the Vía de la Plata. Below: The facade of the Parador, with storks nesting on the chimneys.

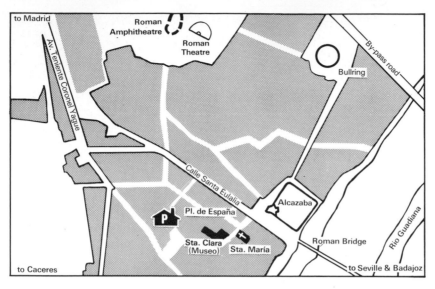

stone blocks and some 100 metres long, and next to it what is probably one of the most beautiful antiquities in Spain—the theatre constructed by Augustus' son-in-law Agrippa in 18 BC. The curving stone terraces with their numerous access tunnels have been restored and are substantially complete. From their steep heights some 5,500 spectators could look down on to a wide stage backed by a graceful colonnade, from whose shadows weatherworn Roman busts frown out at the descendants of the Romano-Iberians, as they pose in the sunshine for a snapshot and then, like the cheering patricians and legionaries, go and are lost.

Mérida was taken by the Moors in 713; and its great *Alcázar* (or castle), now the abode of nesting storks, was built by 'Abd-al-Rahman II of Córdoba in 835, largely with stone blocks fashioned by the Romans. One of the most impressive features is the large carved beam supporting the roof of a stairway leading down to a cistern fed from the neighbouring Guadiana. But it is impossible to get away from the Romans in Mérida; and even the courtyard of the Moorish castle has been converted into an open-air museum. It houses a series of tessellated pavements brought from other parts of the town and the foundations of Roman villas, with the original causeway running alongside, excavated on the site. After the Christian Reconquest in the thirteenth century Mérida passed into the control of the Order of Santiago, but it soon fell into decadence, yielding its pre-eminence as the first city of the Extremadura to Badajoz.

The Parador reflects all these facets of the city's history. Its site was first occupied by the Roman temple of La Concordia; and the white marble columns in the patio with their half-obliterated Arabic inscriptions may date from this period. The temple was replaced

by a Visigoth church, of which there is evidence in the shape of carved capitals; this in turn was destroyed by the Moors. The present elegant Baroque building dates from the foundation in 1602 of the Convento de Jesús by the Order of Santa Clara; but its fortunes, like those of Mérida declined, and before its rehabilitation by the M.I.T. it had done duty as the local jail. The old part of the building centres on a fine interior patio (over which an awning is drawn during the heat of summer); and the bedrooms, which were extended by a new wing in 1966, look on to a cool garden with fountains and topiaried trees in the Moorish style.

43

The Extremadura, or *Extrema Ora* of the Romans, has always been noted for its hams. Times have not much changed since Richard Ford wrote, 'Vast districts of this unreclaimed province are covered with woods of oak, beech, and chestnut; but these parklike scenes have no charm for native eyes; blind to the picturesque, they are only thinking of the number of pigs which can be fattened on the mast and acorns ...' He adds that the capital of the Estremenian pig-districts is Montánchez near Mérida 'and doubtless the hilly spot where ... the Duc de St. Simon ate and admired so much; *"Ces jambons ont un parfum si admirable, un gout si relevé et si vivifiant, qu'on en est surpris: il est impossible de rien manger si exquis."'* The Duke was evidently referring to *Jamón serrano*, dark and highly cured like Bayonne or Parma ham.

This ham is always served as one of the fifteen small dishes making up a Parador *hors d'oeuvres* (virtually a meal in itself and best shared), or it may be eaten thinly sliced, by itself or with slices of melon—in which case one should ask for *Jamón de Jabugo*. It is also used in a range of dishes, such as *Tortilla de jamón* (ham omelette), *Alcachofas con jamón* (artichoke hearts sautéed with ham), *Berenjenas empanadas con jamón* (a fried sandwich of ham and aubergine) or *Truchas a la Navarra* (Navarre-style trout), most of which may be sampled at Mérida. The Parador offers pork in other forms and also an excellent *Gazpacho a la extremeña*, a regional variant of the cold soup so popular in Andalusia.

As remarkable as its hams is a red wine from Montánchez, which grows a *flor* in the manner of Montilla or sherry and is made in the small peasant bodegas of the village with equipment no more elaborate than a few earthenware *tinajas*, an old-fashioned press and a pump. To taste this in Mérida one must try one of the bars off its main street, the Santa Eulalia; the Parador serves sound local wine, red and white, in carafes and also the more sophisticated growths of the neighbouring Castillo de Medellín, in addition to the usual selection of Riojas.

Left and opposite: Tesselated pavements from Roman villas in Mérida.

44

GAZPACHO EXTREMEÑO
COLD SOUP FROM THE EXTREMADURA
Serves 6
2 cloves of garlic, peeled
Salt
2 egg yolks
3oz (100gm) fresh breadcrumbs
4fl oz (120ml) refined olive oil
2 tablespoons vinegar
Pound the cloves of garlic in a mortar with a little salt so as to make a smooth paste. Stir in and thoroughly incorporate the egg yolks and breadcrumbs, then add the olive oil drop by drop as if making a mayonnaise. Transfer to a bowl and slowly stir in $2\frac{1}{2}$ pints ($1\frac{1}{2}$ litres) of water and the vinegar. Check the seasoning and cool in the refrigerator before serving.

TRUCHAS CON JAMON
TROUT WITH HAM
Serves 4
This dish originated in the north of Spain and is often described as *Truchas a la Navarra*.
Olive oil for frying
7oz (200gm) *tocino* or belly of pork, cut up
4 slices ham, about the same size as the trout
4 trout
Salt and pepper
Heat a little olive oil in a pan and fry the belly of pork until it is crisp and has released all its fat. Remove the pork and use for other purposes. In the mixture of oil and fat left in the pan, fry the ham for a few minutes, then transfer it to a pre-heated serving dish. Wash, dry and season the trout with salt and pepper. Make sure that the fat in the pan is still hot and fry the fish until golden, turning them once or twice with a fish slice, but taking care that they do not break.

Place the trout on top of the slices of ham and serve with new potatoes if available.

Alternatively, slit and open the trout when cooked, remove the backbone, insert the slice of ham and fold back the upper half of the fish so as to make a sandwich.

The proscenium of the Roman theatre at Mérida.

MIGAS EXTREMEÑAS

SAVOURY BREADCRUMBS FROM THE EXTREMADURA

Served with fried eggs, these crisp-fried breadcrumbs make a good supper dish.

Stale bread
Salt and pepper
Cayenne pepper
2 cloves of garlic
Olive oil

Leave some stale bread overnight in a bowl to moisten with a little water, to which has been added a pinch of Cayenne pepper and salt.

Heat some olive oil in a frying pan and cook the cloves of garlic until golden, then remove and discard them. Add the moist bread to the hot oil and stir vigorously with a fork so as to break it up into crumbs and continue frying until crisp. Remove with a draining spoon and absorb any excess oil on kitchen paper before serving.

As a variation, first fry a few slices of *chorizo*, remove and reserve them before making the breadcrumbs and arrange around a plate with the savoury breadcrumbs and fried eggs.

46

In 711 the advance party of a Muslim army under Tariq ibn-Ziyad crossed the Strait of Gibraltar into Spain. The incursion marked the latest stage of an Arab thrust along the North African coast, which had begun with the annexation of Egypt in 642 by the second of the Umayyad caliphs of Damascus, 'Umar. For the three hundred years since the break-up of the Roman Empire in the early fifth century Spain had been ruled by the Visigoths, one of a number of northern tribes which had invaded the country by way of the Pyrenees. Their last king, Roderick, was soundly defeated by Tariq; and during the next few years the Moors, of mixed Arab and Berber descent, fanned out across the Peninsula, occupying most of the country apart from Galicia and Asturias and the Basque area in the north-east. It was from the north that King Alfonso I of Asturias mounted the first serious Christian counter-attack from 739 to 757; but three centuries were to pass before the Reconquest made any further impact on Moorish al-Andalus, whose northern border was roughly marked by the River Duero.

The rapid occupation of most of the Peninsula (including present-day Portugal) by the Moors and their predominance for a period of some five hundred years was more than an interruption in the country's evolution and has differentiated Spain from any of the other Western European countries born of the dissolution of the Roman Empire. The Reconquest was the perennial theme of Spanish history until the fall of the last Moorish stronghold, the emirate of Granada, to the Catholic Monarchs in 1492. Spanish thought and the language itself were profoundly influenced by the Moors; and especially in the south the effects are still to be seen in architecture and social customs: many of the Adalusians are directly descended from the Muslim invaders.

The most resplendent period of Moorish domination, lasting until the beginning of the eleventh century, was that of the Umayyad emirs and caliphs of Córdoba, of whom the first was 'Abd-al-Rahman I, a refugee from Syria.

Marqués de Villena: Alarcón

The Castle of Alarcón, lying off the main road and roughly half way between Madrid and Valencia, and now the Parador of the Marqués de Villena, was built early during the Muslim period, since in 785 it was the scene for the murder of a Moor known as 'The Blind One'. Together with the village behind (once a fortified town of 12,000 inhabitants), it perches on a crag islanded in the gorge of the River Júcar and is approachable only by a narrow road winding up from the valley below. The strategic importance of the site was recognized by the Romans, from whom it was wrested by a son of the Visigothic King Alarico—hence its name. The elaborate system of outlying watch-towers, gateways built across the track and curtain walls guarding the precipitous heights (still largely intact) made it almost impregnable in Moorish times; and the castle was one of the principal bastions of the rebellion of 'Umar ibn-Hafsun during the hey-day of the Córdoban caliphate.

Ibn-Hafsun was a man with an eye for a defensive position, and from his mountain lair of Bobastro in the Serranía de Ronda to

Left: The approach to the Parador of the Marqués de Villena.

the south he engaged in a Robin Hood career of brigandage. His depredations grew to such an extent that various expeditions were despatched against him from Córdoba, but he survived a full-scale attack in 888, when the emir al-Mundhir died suddenly during the siege (probably poisoned by his brother and successor 'Abd-Allah) and by 891 was battering on the gates of Córdoba itself. It was not until after his death in 917 that the greatest of the Córdoban caliphs, 'Abd-al-Rahman III, quelled the revolt and with less than his usual magnanimity had the body of the old rebel exhumed and crucified.

Alarcón fell to Alfonso VI of Castile in 1085, only to be recaptured by the Moors. Alfonso VIII ordered an all-out attack in 1184; and the legend goes that, after a fruitless siege of nine months, his commander, Fernán Martín de Ceballos, scaled the walls by sticking a couple of swords into the cement in the manner of rock-climbers' spikes, climbing up and leading the assault party in person. The year 1184 was thereafter known as the 'Year of Alarcón'.

The castle was subsequently given to the Order of St. James and was a rallying point for the forces which defeated the third and last waves of Moorish invaders from Africa, the Almohads, at the Battle of Las Navas de Tolosa in 1212, so presaging the end of the Muslim domination of Spain.

Among the later possessors of Alarcón, which continued to play an important role in the internal struggles of the thirteenth, fourteenth and fifteenth centuries, one may single out Juan Pacheco, Marqués de Villena, who has given his name to the Parador. Pacheco was an inveterate and ambitious conspirator, who, despite

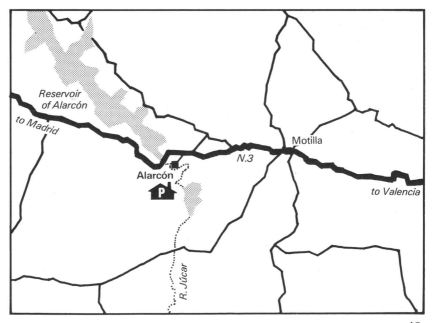

49

his devious behaviour became the favourite of Henry IV of Castile (1454–74) and was not only created Master of the Order of Santiago but given a string of properties from Toledo to Murcia, among them the Castle of Alarcón. During the manoeuvring which preceded the accession of Isabel the Catholic to the throne of Castile, he supported the claim of Henry's supposedly bastard daughter, Juana la Beltraneja, and was subsequently stripped of many of his possessions, but left with Alarcón, which long remained in the Pacheco family.

The castle was in ruinous condition when taken over and restored by the M.I.T.; and the Parador has been installed in the main keep (which is now occupied by bedrooms and a lift) and in the other buildings surrounding the central courtyard, with its old well and spreading fig tree.

The village, a few minutes' walk from the gates, is a place of narrow cobbled streets and low white houses, interspersed with deserted baronial mansions bearing the noble stone escutcheons of their former owners. Its five churches, most of them locked and abandoned, testify to departed glories; and that of Santiago and Santa María is notable for its intricate plateresque facade adorned with splendid sixteenth-century statuary.

The courtyard of the Parador of the Marqués de Villena.

50

The dining room of the Parador is one of the original great halls of the castle: the stonework has been left bare; and at one end there is a large and beautiful mediaeval painting in glowing reds, oranges and golds of the Last Supper. The waitresses wear embroidered regional costume, of which a feature is the thick white lace stockings.

Alarcón lies in Manchuela, the northeastern part of the great plateau of La Mancha, stretching south from Madrid and the scene of Don Quixote's adventures. This is reflected in the many regional dishes listed in the menu, such as *Ensalada manchega*, a salad given piquancy by a sprinkling of flaked *bacalao* (the dried and salted cod so popular in Spain and Portugal); *Tortilla guisada* ('stewed omelette'), a surprisingly appetizing version of the Spanish potato omelette; *Pisto manchego*, a variant on *ratatouille*, made with courgettes, green peppers and tomatoes; *Perdiz escabechada*, marinated partridge; *Cordero en caldereta*, a ragout of lamb in a sauce prepared from the livers; *Morteruelo*, a fricassé of pigs' livers; and *Natillas con pestiños*, honeyed fritters served with custard.

La Mancha, of which Manchuela is an extension, is the largest wine-growing area in Spain and supplies vast amounts of fresh and reliable carafe wine, loosely called Valdepeñas, to other less favoured parts of the country. The Parador lists a local 'Castillo de Alarcón', red and white, and also *jarras* (carafes) of the '*blanco y tinto de la tierra*', in fact from Utiel-Requena on the Valencian border. Wines such as these are considerably better in quality and more individual than a comparable French *vin ordinaire*.

ENSALADA MANCHEGA
SALAD FROM LA MANCHA
Serves 6
Salad
1 7½oz (200gm) tin of tuna
2 hard-boiled eggs, sliced
4 tomatoes, blanched, peeled and cut up
1 onion, finely chopped
12 olives, green or black, stoned
1oz (30gm) *bacalao* (dried and salted cod)

Prepare the *bacalao* by soaking it overnight, draining, drying and flaking it.

Drain the oil from the tuna, flake it with a fork, then mix it with the hard-boiled egg in a salad bowl. Continue by adding the tomatoes— which will be a little wet after blanching and cutting up—the onion, olives and prepared *bacalao*.

Dressing
4 dessertspoons refined olive oil
2 dessertspoons vinegar or lemon juice
¼ teaspoon French mustard
1 clove of garlic, squeezed
Salt and pepper

Make the dressing by stirring together all the ingredients, pour it over the salad and toss thoroughly.

TORTILLA GUISADA
SPANISH OMELETTE IN PIQUANT SAUCE
Serves 2
Omelette
¾lb (340gm) potatoes, cut up
1 medium-sized onion, cut up
5fl oz (1½dl) olive oil
6 eggs
Salt

Get the oil really hot in a frying pan, then add the potatoes and onion.
Reduce the heat, cover the pan with a lid and cook slowly for ½ hour
until the contents are soft. Season with salt and remove with a draining
spoon, reserving any excess oil for further use. Meanwhile beat the
eggs in a bowl. Add the cooked potato and onion and return the
mixture to the pan, first cleaning it and adding a little of the reserved
oil. Cook for a few minutes, shaking vigorously when the contents
begin to steam, then place a large plate above the pan and invert the
half-cooked omelette on to it. Slide back into the pan without adding
further oil, so as to cook the second side, and turn out on to a plate.

Sauce
Olive oil
1 small onion, finely chopped
1 dessertspoon sweet paprika
1 level dessertspoon flour
A little chopped parsley
1 clove of garlic, crushed
Salt

To make the sauce, heat the remainder of the oil in a frying pan and fry
the onion for 10 or 15 minutes until golden. Stir in the sweet paprika,
the flour, parsley and garlic, then add ½ pint (3dl) of water and a little
salt. Leave to cook together for a few minutes, then put the omelette in
a *cazuela* or stew pan, pour the glowing red sauce on top, and cook
slowly for 10 minutes before serving.

Left: The Castle of Alarcón
(from a nineteenth-century engraving). Opposite: Old houses
in the township of Alarcón.

After the first decades of the invasion from North Africa, when the Moors advanced along the Mediterranean coast of Spain and struck deep into France across the Pyrenees, to be thrown back by Charles Martel in 732, the northeastern corner of the Peninsula went its own way. Not content with expelling the Moors from the southwestern tip of France, the Franks struck back across the Pyrenees. It was thus that Charlemagne undertook his ambitious expedition against Saragossa, culminating in the disastrous ambush of his rearguard at Roncesvalles in 778, immortalized by the Chanson de Roland.

By the end of his reign Charlemagne had reoccupied Gerona; and his son Louis the Pious took Barcelona and campaigned as far south as Tortosa on the delta of the Ebro. These successes were achieved with the active cooperation of the indigenous inhabitants of the region; and in their voluntary acceptance of Carolingian suzerainty was founded the Marca Hispánica *(or Spanish Mark), which was the genesis of an independent Catalonia.*

Charlemagne had not exacted the same strict conditions of surrender as he had for territories conquered by the Franks by force of arms; and although the counts of the various regions were first appointed directly by the Frankish kings, in course of time their offices became hereditary. The detachment of the Spanish Mark from the Empire came about not as the result of violent rebellion or an upsurge of nationalistic feeling, but more by default; and in founding the House of Barcelona, Guifré el Pilós (Wilfred the Hairy) instituted a dynasty which was to shape the country's destinies for the next three centuries.

56

Duques de Cardona: Cardona

The Castle of Cardona in the foothills of the Pyrenees northwest of Barcelona, which has recently been restored by the M.I.T. and opened as the Parador of Cardona, will always be associated with this turning point in the history of Catalonia. It was first built by Louis the Pious in 789 as a central strongpoint to secure the territories wrested from the Moors and about a century later was extended and strengthened by Wilfred. From this period dates the picturesque legend, according to which Wilfred, while fighting against the Moors at the side of Louis' successor Charles the Bald, was wounded. By dipping four fingers into his blood and drawing them across Wilfred's gilded shield, the king made a grant of arms, which was the origin of the Catalan flag with its red bars on a yellow ground. It would be naive to read into this story the recognition by the Franks of an independent Catalonia, although by his death in 897 Wilfred had achieved the *de facto* separation of the principality from the Empire.

Not long after the refortification by Wilfred, the governorship of the castle went to Ramón Folch, a nephew of the Emperor

Previous page: A corridor in the Parador of the Vía de la Plata before reconstruction. Opposite above: The approach to the Parador of the Marqués de Villena. Opposite below: The courtyard of the same Parador. Right: The Parador of Cardona.

Charlemagne. He was ennobled by Wilfred as Viscount of Cardona, and in 1375 his descendants were elevated first to Counts, and later to Dukes of Cardona.

Such was its strength that the castle remained impregnable for centuries: in 1711, during the War of the Spanish Succession, it was unsuccessfully stormed by French and Spanish troops under the Count of Mauret; and at the time of the Peninsular War, General Lacy successfully defended it against Marshal Suchet in 1811. In the ensuing civil war it successfully resisted repeated attacks by the Carlists.

The castle stands solidly on a conical hill rising above the little walled town of Cardona. During the recent reconstruction the eleventh-century Church of San Vicente, standing within the fortified precinct, has been carefully restored. Among its twenty-two tombs, it contains those of the first Duke of Cardona and his wife, Francisca Manrique de Lara, the work of a gifted but unknown sculptor of the sixteenth century. The beautiful Gothic courtyard and various of the interior apartments have also been renovated.

The Parador is well-placed for a visit to the Monastery of Santa María de Ripoll, which was rebuilt by Wilfred the Hairy in 888 after its destruction by the Moors. He was later buried there; and it became a cradle of the arts and sciences in Catalonia. It is also within easy reach of Barcelona, whose reputation as a centre of commerce and industry sometimes obscures its other attractions. The Museums of Catalan Art and Archaeology, the old quarter around the Cathedral, the *Ramblas* with their glowing flower stalls and the port area and excellent fish restaurants are all worth the visit.

Above: Guifré el Pilós (Wilfred the Hairy), who by founding the House of Barcelona paved the way for the future expansion of Catalonia and the Crown of Aragon during the Middle Ages (from the genealogical tree of the Counts of Barcelona at the Monastery of Poblet).

Left: The Gothic courtyard of the Parador of Cardona.

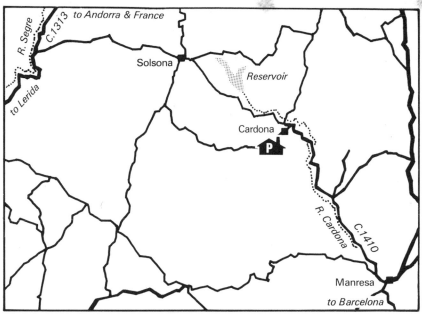

Catalonia enjoys one of the most varied cuisines in the Peninsula. The region is the home of one of the best-known Spanish sauces, *Ali-oli*, a mayonnaise rich in garlic, which has been famed for its culinary and medicinal properties since the times of Virgil—who knew it as *moretum*. For those who are not afraid of garlic, it goes excellently with fish cooked as *Bullabesa*, or Catalan-style *bouillabaisse*, and served separately from the broth. Another fish dish, which originated in Catalonia but is now served all over Spain, is the *Zarzuela de mariscos* (see also page 34). The lobsters and other shellfish from the Costa Brava are deservedly famous, as are the cured hams and sausages from Vich in the Pyrenees. Of these one of the favourites is *Butifarra*, which with *Mongetes* (a variety of chick pea) is the main ingredient of *Butifarra amb mongetes*. The typical Catalan way of preparing chicken is *en Chanfaina*, a rich sauce containing tomatoes, onions, aubergines and peppers, as well as white wine and a variety of spices and flavourings. Among the best of the sweets is *Crema quemada a la catalana*, an entirely individual version of cream caramel with a thin and brittle film of caramel on the surface.

Catalonia has been making wines since Roman time. Its choice growths include: Alella, a soft and fruity wine, available both red and white, from ancient vineyards just north of Barcelona; Priorato, typically full-bodied, strong in alcohol and often almost black in colour; and Panadés, where the Bodegas Torres, using the traditional techniques of Bordeaux, make some of the best table wine in Spain, both red and white. The Panadés area, south of Barcelona, also produces the best sparkling wine in Spain. Although made by the traditional *méthode champenoise*, these *espumosos* may not be labelled 'Champagne'—but those from firms like Codorniú, the Conde de Caralt and the Bodegas Bilbaínas (its excellent 'Royal Carlton' is in fact made in the Rioja) are first-rate sparkling wines. To complete the gamut, the pleasant coastal resort of Sitges has long been known for its dessert wines.

The largest producer of wines in the area is Tarragona. The wine is

in fact brought there from further afield by tanker and blended in its
great bodegas, mainly for export as 'Spanish Burgundy' or 'Spanish
Chablis'. The historic old town, with its impressive Roman remains
and beautiful Gothic cathedral, also produces a variety of internationally
known vermouths under licence and makes Chartreuse under the
supervision of the Carthusians from Grenoble.

While in this area, no wine-lover should miss a visit to Villafranca
del Panadés on the main road south from Barcelona, which possesses
one of the best and most comprehensive wine museums in the world.

ZARZUELA DE MARISCOS
Serves 6
Olive oil
1 onion, finely chopped
11oz (300gm) conger eel, sliced
7oz (200gm) inkfish, cleaned and cut up
11oz (300gm) angler fish, sliced
7oz (200gm) hake or rock bass, sliced
8oz (225gm) peeled prawns
6 large prawns in shell
1 clove of garlic, crushed
A little tomato paste
2 glasses dry white wine
Ground parsley
Salt and pepper
12 clams
Ground saffron
Clean, wash and dry the whitefish. Boil the clams until they open, and
reserve. Heat some olive oil in a *cazuela* or stew pan and fry the onion
for about 10 minutes until golden, then add the conger eel, inkfish,
angler fish, hake or rock bass, and the prawns, peeled and in shell.
Stir in the garlic, tomato paste and white wine, then season with salt,
pepper and parsley. Cook together slowly for 20 minutes, adding the
clams and saffron after 10 minutes.

This dish can be made with any available whitefish, provided that it
is firm and does not disintegrate during cooking.

PARRILLADA DE PESCADO CON SALSA ROMESCO
MIXED GRILL OF FISH WITH ROMESCO SAUCE
Serves 4
Fish
4 sea crayfish or large prawns ⎫
4 prawns   ⎬ in the shell
8 mussels   ⎪
8 clams   ⎭
4 medium slices of bass
4 red mullet
4 slices of hake
Salt
Olive oil
All the fish is simply sprinkled with a little olive oil and grilled. In this
part of Spain this is done over charcoal. It is served with the following
sauce on the side.

Opposite above: One of the
battlements of the Parador of
Cardona. Opposite below: The
Parador's bar installed in an
old dungeon.

61

Sauce

This sauce was christened after the Catalan name of the pimientos used in making it.

3 tomatoes, blanched, peeled and freed from pips
3 cloves of garlic
3 dried pimientos *Romesco* or chillis
10 roasted almonds
1 slice fried bread
Pinch of white pepper
4fl oz (120ml) refined olive oil
4fl oz (120ml) vinegar

Grill the tomatoes and garlic until browned and reserve. Soak the dried pimientos in tepid water and remove the pips, then grind them with the almonds in a mortar. Mix thoroughly with the garlic, tomatoes, fried bread and pepper, so as to make a smooth paste. Transfer to a bowl and add the oil gradually, stirring with a wooden spoon as if making mayonnaise. Finally, beat in the vinegar and season with salt. Cover the sauce and cool in the refrigerator for two hours, then pass it through a sieve, check the seasoning and beat well before serving.

This sauce is also delicious with vegetables, other fish and grilled meat.

62

What supplied the dynamic for the Reconquest of the Moorish-held territories and inspired the Christians of the north with a will to win was the Christian faith itself, and in particular the cult of Santiago (St. James), the patron saint of Spain. There is a legend that, as early as 939, he materialized on the field of Simancas, inspiring Ramiro II of León and his men to overthrow the mighty 'Abd-al-Rahman III himself.

According to tradition, the remains of St. James the Apostle were buried at Santiago de Compostela (the word is a garbled form of campus stellae *or 'the field of the star') in Galicia, the furthest point of his missionary travels. From the time when Archbishop Godescalco visited the shrine in 950 with a group of French pilgrims, and under the influence of the Benedictines from Cluny who built a cathedral there, the pilgrimage to Santiago became the most famous in Europe. Besides heartening the Spanish Christians in their centuries' long fight against the Moors, this new contact with her neighbours was henceforth to cause Spain to look to France and Western Europe for her cultural renaissance, rather than to al-Andalus and Islam.*

The Cluniacs, who moved into Spain in strength and with their Burgundian confrères were in due course to play an important role in the emergence of an independent Portugal, set up a network of churches, hospices and hospitals for the use of the great army of pilgrims. Starting from Paris, Vézelay, Le Puy and Arles, the pilgrim routes crossed the Pyrenees and converged at Puente de la Reina near Pamplona. The Calzada, *or paved way, was one of the first new roads to be built in Spain since the time of the Romans.*

Santo Domingo de la Calzada: Santo Domingo de la Calzada

Typical of the hospices was that of Santo Domingo de la Calzada, in the hills west of Logroño, now a Parador of the M.I.T. The little town sprang up during the eleventh century to serve the scallop-shelled pilgrims using the Roman road from Logroño to Burgos. Santo Domingo (St. Dominic) de la Calzada, born in 1109, from whom it took its name, devoted his life to improving their lot. Because of the thick forests and the difficulties of fording the Najerilla and Oja rivers, the going was hard; the Saint built bridges and laid out the stone causeway or *calzada*, completing his work by the construction of the hospice and hospital. It was built on the site of a former palace of the Kings of Navarre and taken under the wing of Pope Honorius III in 1216, later fulfilling the functions of a monastery and a residence for lay brothers dedicated to alleviating the sufferings of the poor.

The building retains mediaeval features, notably the splendid arched hall with stained glass ceiling, now used as the lounge. Across the square is the original church used by St. Dominic, raised to the rank of cathedral in 1235 and extended and renovated in the

Below: The mediaeval hall in the Parador of Santo Domingo de la Calzada, now the lounge.

The castle of Cuzcurrita near Santo Domingo, whose vineyards produce a superior chateau-bottled Rioja.

fifteenth and eighteenth centuries. His tomb inside incorporates a statue of the Saint, flanked by those of a cock and a hen; and high on the wall opposite is a cage containing two live birds. These commemorate a strange legend. The hostess of a local inn fell in love with a young pilgrim, en route for Santiago with his parents; and when he refused her advances hid some valuable goblets among his belongings. They were discovered, and the young man, less fortunate than Joseph, was hung from a gibbet. The bereaved parents, to whom he appeared in a vision, went to the *corregidor*, only to be told that their son was as dead as the fowl on the table in front of him; at which point the birds sprang up and began singing. The young pilgrim was then discovered, still miraculously alive.

The town conserves other historic churches, seignorial palaces and a stretch of its mediaeval walls, dating from the reign of Pedro the Cruel of Castile during the fourteenth century. It is also a convenient point from which to visit the adjacent town of Nájera, famous for the monastery church of Santa María, which contains the splendidly sculptured tombs of many of the kings and queens of Navarre. There is no Parador at Santiago de Compostela, the goal of the pilgrimage; but its great cathedral embodying the shrine of St. James is certainly worth the visit; and the privately owned Hotel Reyes Cátolicos, installed in a splendid sixteenth-century palace, is one of the best in Spain.

66

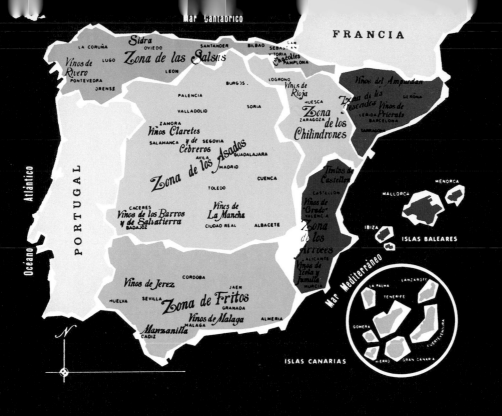

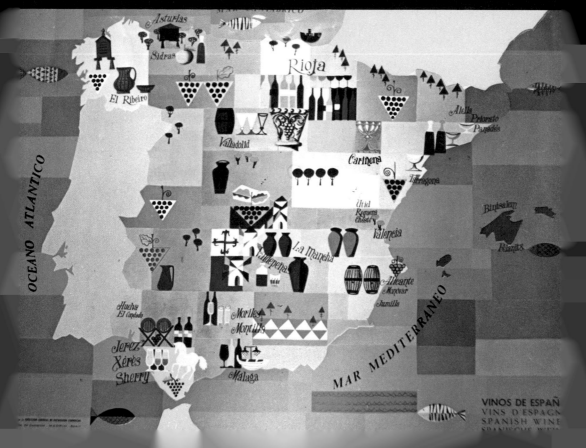

Left: *Mirador* in the Parador of the Condes de Alba y Aliste. Below: The Parador of Monzón de los Campos.

Right: Pilgrims on the road to Santiago de Compostela (from an engraving by H. Cock after Breughel).

Below: The old Rioja mark.

Below: The Rioja seal, a guarantee of origin appearing on all bottles of genuine Rioja wine.

The Parador of Santo Domingo de la Calzada is on the northern fringe of the Rioja, which, apart from the best-known table wines in Spain, also produces vegetables in abundance. Any meal might well begin with the luscious asparagus. The *Menestra de verduras* is an excellent dish of mixed vegetables; and the *Pimientos rellenos* are a savoury version of stuffed peppers, filled in the Rioja with a mixture of seasoned bread-crumbs and a little minced meat and then stewed in sauce. The locally grown haricot beans (*alubias* or *caparón*) are particularly good and are served at the Parador with quail. Perhaps the most famous regional dish is *Lechazo asado* (milk-fed lamb, unknown in England and roasted in a baker's oven), best eaten at the plain deal tables of Terete in near-by Haro, a restaurant much patronized by the *bodegeros*.

Haro is the headquarters of the Rioja Alta, the best of the region's famous wine-growing districts, which date from Roman times and also

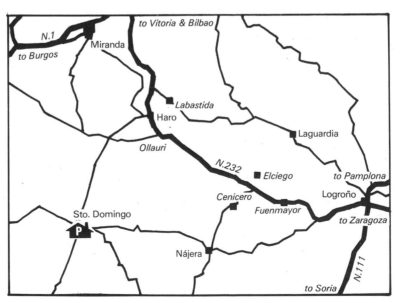

comprise the Rioja Alavesa further north and the Rioja Baja to the east. The Parador, half an hour's drive from Haro, is an excellent centre for visiting the bodegas—the whole area, about 100km long and 40km wide, lying along the Ebro valley, is comparatively small. Individual bodegas—to mention at random only such well-known names as López de Heredia, Bilbaínas, Santiago, the Marqués de Riscal or Paternina— welcome visits, ending with a tasting of their wines.

Rioja differs from vintage French wines in being matured for much longer periods in oak casks. Anything bearing the official stamp of the *Consejo Regulador* on the label must be aged in wood for at least two years and may be chosen with confidence; and the old reserves, like the 1934 Castillo de Ygay from the Marqués de Murrieta, can hold their own with the choice growths from Bordeaux and Burgundy. The fruity white wines may be either dry (*seco*) or sweet (*dulce*), and the reds correspond very roughly to clarets (*clarete*) or burgundies.

As one would expect of a wine-growing district, the carafe wine served in the Parador is of excellent quality.

Above: The Cathedral of Santo Domingo de la Calzada.

MENESTRA DE VERDURAS A LA RIOJANA
MIXED VEGETABLES FROM THE RIOJA
Serves 6
This dish somewhat resembles a *ratatouille*.
1lb (½kg) broad beans, shelled
7oz (200gm) garden peas, shelled
1 onion, finely chopped
2oz (60gm) belly of pork, cut up
2oz (60gm) cooked ham, cut up
2 bay leaves
2 large tomatoes, blanched
1 clove of garlic, peeled
Saffron
Black pepper, freshly ground
Salt
2 hardboiled eggs, sliced

Cook the beans and peas separately for 15 minutes each, drain and reserve in a bowl. Heat some olive oil in a pan and fry the onion for about 10 minutes with the belly of pork, ham and bay leaves. Add the wine, reduce the heat a little, then stir in the tomatoes with a wooden spoon so as to break them up. Now add the cooked beans and peas, mixing them in well. Meanwhile grind the garlic, a little saffron and the pepper in a mortar with a teaspoon of water. Stir into the contents of the pan and season with salt. Leave over a slow fire for about 10 minutes, taking care that the mixture does not stick, as there is now very little liquid. Arrange in a serving dish surrounded by the slices of hard-boiled egg.

PIMIENTOS RELLENOS A LA RIOJANA
STUFFED PEPPERS FROM THE RIOJA
Serves 4
1lb (½kg) minced pork
4 eggs
Pinch of nutmeg
Pinch of freshly ground pepper

70

1 clove of garlic, finely chopped or squeezed
A little chopped parsley
Salt
8 baked pimientos (or equivalent from a can)
Flour for coating
Olive oil
2 onions, chopped
1 teaspoon sweet paprika
1 dessertspoon flour
½ pint (3dl) broth (or if unavailable, water)

Thoroughly mix the minced pork with two beaten eggs, the nutmeg, pepper, garlic, parsley and a little salt. If using fresh baked pimientos, cut them at the top and remove the capsule and seeds. Canned peppers should be held carefully in the palm of the hand when stuffing them, so that they do not fall apart. Fill in the stuffing with a teaspoon and secure the open end with a toothpick. Beat the remaining two eggs and dredge the pimientos first in the beaten egg and then in flour; fry and then lay them carefully in a *cazuela* or stew pan, which if possible should be large enough to avoid putting one on top of another.

Heat a little olive oil in a pan and fry the onions for about 15 minutes, stir in the paprika, the dessertspoon of flour and the broth or water, and cook for five minutes. Now pour the sauce over the pimientos and leave them over a very low heat for ½ hour.

71

In July 997, al-Mansur the Victorious, who had effectively usurped the powers of the caliph, rode out of Córdoba at the head of a large army. Crossing what is now Portugal, he descended upon Santiago de Compostela on August 10th. The inhabitants had fled the city, which, with its cathedral, was razed to the ground. Al-Mansur spared only the actual tomb of St. James—Christians, after all, were 'People of the Book' like Muslims. On his return march to Córdoba he carried off a great train of captives, together with the bells and doors of the shattered cathedral. The beams were used for additions to the Great Mosque; the bells were later restored to Santiago after the fall of Córdoba to the Christians.

But the Córdoban caliphate had burnt itself out; the spectacular successes of al-Mansur were the last glittering burst of a rocket against the night sky. The caliphate broke up in 1031, and Moorish al-Andalus fragmented into the small principalities of the 'party kings' (reyes de taifas), which came under increasing attack from the Christian kingdoms of the north, culminating in the recapture of Toledo by King Alfonso VI of Castile in 1085 and the fall of Valencia to his friend and enemy El Cid in 1094. This was nevertheless only the beginning of the Reconquest proper, since further waves of Berber invaders, the Almoravids and the Almohads, were to prolong the Moorish domination of the south for another two centuries, until the last of the Almohad caliphs, Muhammad al-Nasir, was overthrown at the Battle of Las Navas de Tolosa in the Sierra Morena, north of Córdoba, in 1212.

At the same time there was a tendency for the independent Christian kingdoms, like León-Asturias, Castile and Navarre, which often joined forces against the Moors, to combine under a single ruler. Because of the habit of their kings to redivide their possessions among their sons, who would sometimes fight more bitterly among themselves than against the Moors, Spain was not finally unified until 1479, when Castile and the Crown of Aragon, then a Mediterranean power in its own right, were united under the Catholic Monarchs, Isabel and Ferdinand.

Castillo de Monzón: Monzón de los Campos

Some of the most vicious of this infighting among the Christians took place in the meadows of Carrión, north of Palencia and near the castle which has very recently been restored by M.I.T. as the Parador of Monzón de Campos.

On his death in 1065, Ferdinand I, who had made significant inroads into al-Andalus, divided his realms of Castile, León and Galicia among his three sons. The youngest was soon deprived of Galicia by his brothers, Sancho II of Castile and Alfonso of León (later to become Alfonso VI of León and Castile), who then fought between themselves for the remainder.

Early in 1072 their armies clashed at Golpejera. According to the *romances*, each army managed to capture the monarch on the opposing side. Fourteen Leonese knights were escorting Sancho from the field, when they were attacked single-handed by his renowned *alférez* (or marshal), El Cid, Rodrigo Díaz, who by rescuing Sancho so demoralized the Leonese that their army turned and fled. Whatever the actual details, Alfonso was captured and imprisoned in the castle of Burgos, from which he was released at the intercession of his sister doña Urraca and found exile at the court of King Ma'mun of Toledo. Sancho was meanwhile crowned

The Parador of the Castillo de Monzón.

73

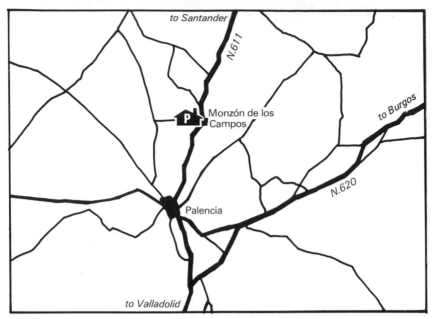

King-Emperor of León; but there was to be a further dramatic twist, as will appear shortly.

The fortifications of the castle of Monzón de Campos—so-called to distinguish it from Monzón in Aragon—originally extended on both sides of the River Carrión, on whose banks the battle was fought. Only one group of buildings now survives. At the time of the Cid it belonged to Pedro Ansúrez, a scion of his bitter opponents, the Counts of Carrión—according to legend two younger members of the family, the *Infantes* of Carrión, later married and abandoned the Cid's daughters, having first stripped them naked and whipped them. Whatever the truth of this, Monzón had been a place of great strategic importance since the time of the great Alfonso III of Asturias in the tenth century and had long played a role in the history of Castile. In 1029 a marriage was planned between the last Count of Castile, García II, and Sancha, daughter of Vermudo III of León. On his way to the betrothal ceremony, the ten-year-old count was murdered on the steps of the Church of San Juan in León by the three Vela brothers, who subsequently took refuge in Monzón, only to meet terrible retribution at the hands of García's brother-in-law, Sancho the Great of Navarre.

> *En Monzón los han cercado*
> *prenieron a todos tres*
> *vivos los habían quemado*

Although Sancho had the assassins burnt alive outside the castle, his own part in the outrage is suspect, since he promptly improved the occasion to possess himself of Castile.

74

Above: King Alfonso VI and his evil counsellors (from the *Crónica del Cid*, 1498).

In 1109 the children of another doña Urraca, daughter of Alfonso VI, found sanctuary in the castle after the break-up of her marriage with Alfonso *el Batallador* of Aragon, as did her lover, don Pedro de Lara, two years later.

The present structure dates from the fourteenth century, when Monzón came into the possession of the Rojas, the Marquesses of Pozo, one of whom married the famous Admiral of Castile, don Alfonso Enríques.

A short drive north from the Parador, off the main road to Santander, lies the old walled town of Carrión de los Condes. It was in the church of Santa María del Camino, a Romanesque building with a strange facade decorated with bulls' heads, that Alfonso is said to have found brief respite after his defeat at Golpejera. Another interesting excursion, to the south, is to Palencia, where Alfonso VIII founded the first university in Spain in 1208. Palencia is also the site of a fine cathedral built between 1321 and 1516.

Right: The Cid, who won one of his most famous battles near Monzón, rides out in exile. (Title-page of the *Crónica del Cid*, 1498.) Below: The *Infantes* of Carrion humiliate their newly-wed wives, the daughters of the Cid (from the *Crónica del Cid*, 1498).

On gastronomic maps of Spain, Old Castile is often designated *La Zona de los Asados* (the region of roasts), so that this is a place to try the *Cordero asado* (roast lamb), at its most delicious in the form of *Lechazo* as already mentioned, or the tender *Cochinillo* (sucking pig). The hilly country rising to the mountain barrier in the north which divides Asturias from the rest of Spain, abounds in game. The *cocidos*, nourishing stews containing chick peas, meat and other vegetables are a staple here as in Castile generally. The region produces a good cheese from Burgos, which is worth asking for as an alternative to the more familiar and generally available *Manchego*.

75

The immediate locality does not produce any wine of note; but this is perhaps the place to mention Vega Sicilia, which makes some of the best, if not *the* best table wine in Spain. Small and entirely uncharacteristic of the region as a whole, the bodega and vineyards lie on the road from Valladolid (60km south) to Soria, on the verges of the River Duero. After the native wines had been destroyed by phylloxera towards the end of the nineteenth century, the vineyards were replanted with French vines. They have been carefully replaced ever since by grafting shoots on American stocks in the bodega's nurseries; and the wines are now made from an admixture of these grapes and native varieties, such as Garnacho. The wines are matured in oak for exceptional periods and are velvety, deep in colour and intensely fruity in flavour. Production is so limited that they sell at a premium; and the better-known restaurants, hotels and Paradores are strictly rationed. Vega Sicilia and its 'baby brother' Valbuena (matured for a somewhat shorter period) are expensive wines by any standard; but no connoisseur of fine wines should leave Spain without tasting a bottle.

CORDERO ASADO AL ESTILO DE CASTILLA
ROAST BABY LAMB CASTILIAN STYLE
This is lamb at its most tender and succulent. It must be cooked with milk-fed lamb, not generally available outside Spain.
Serves 6 to 7
Half of a *Lechazo* or milk-fed lamb
Salt and pepper
Season the lamb with salt and place in a baking tin, with half a glass of water. Preheat the oven to 400°F, Mark 6 and roast for 20 minutes per pound ($\frac{1}{2}$kg) until browned on both sides. The lamb must be turned at intervals and basted with its juice.

Serve with puréed or fried potatoes.

Left: A lounge in the Parador of the Castillo de Monzón. Opposite: The entrance of the Parador.

76

PERDICES ESTOFADAS
STEWED PARTRIDGES WITH CHOCOLATE
Serves 2
2 partridges of 1lb ($\frac{1}{2}$kg) or 1 of 2lb (1kg)
1 onion, cut up
1 head of garlic, whole
1 clove
1 bay leaf
Olive oil
1$\frac{1}{2}$ glasses dry white wine
$\frac{1}{2}$ glass vinegar
1oz (30gm) cooking chocolate, grated
Put the partridge or partridges into an earthenware pot or a stewpan, together with the onion, the head of garlic into which is inserted the clove, the bay leaf, a little olive oil, the wine, vinegar, and salt and pepper. Bring to the boil and then simmer for $\frac{3}{4}$ hr if using two small partridges or 1 hour for a single larger bird. Shake the pot at intervals.

Remove the partridges and place on a heated serving dish and then stir the chocolate into the sauce in the stewpan, leaving it to simmer for a further 10 minutes. Meanwhile arrange fried sliced potatoes around the edge of the serving dish. Finally, rub the sauce through a sieve with a wooden spoon and pour it over the partridges and potatoes.

Opposite: A lounge in the Parador of the Castillo de Monzón.

Opposite: A carved arch in the Castillo de Monzón. Left: The Parador of the Castillo de Monzón.

78

The feud between Sancho II and his brother did not end with Alfonso's exile to Moorish Toledo. During his enforced absence a faction of the Leonese nobility, in particular Pedro Ansúrez and the Beni Gomez family of Carrión, refused to accept Sancho II as their king. Alfonso's sister, doña Urraca, who had worked ceaselessly on his behalf, put herself at the head of the rebels and shut herself up in the stronghold of Zamora, which had earlier been given to her by Alfonso and was deep in the territory of the Counts of Carrión. It was here that the next act of the drama was played out.

Condes de Alba y Aliste: Zamora

The city of Zamora, the site of the Parador of the Condes de Alba y Aliste, lay in a virtually impregnable position, protected both by its massive walls and a sweep of the River Duero; even al-Mansur had been unable to take it. The besieging army was again under command of the Cid; but according to the *romances* he had little stomach for this fratricidal strife and even quarrelled with Sancho on the issue. Be this as it may, the siege was closely pursued; and the motto of Zamora, visible on many a carved stone shield, runs *Zamora no se ganó en una hora* ('Zamora was not won in an hour'). On Sunday, 7 October 1072, one Vellido Adolfo treacherously slipped out of the walls by a postern gate and stabbed Sancho to death in his tent. Alfonso thereupon returned to become King of Castile, and by the famous oath of Santa Gadea, sworn three times in the presence of the Cid, pledged himself innocent of his brother's death. The episode left a bitter taste; and it was not long before the Cid was required to ride out of Burgos with his company to begin his life-long exile from Castile. Alfonso VI and the freebooting Cid were the twin architects of Reconquest during the latter part of the eleventh century; but their disastrous division much impeded its progress.

The twelfth-century gateway of doña Urraca, with its narrow arch and two stout towers, through which one passes on the way to the Parador, still bears the inscription *Afuera! Afuera! Rodrigo, el soberbio castellano* ('Away! Away! Rodrigo, the proud Castilian') and an even earlier building by the city walls near the River Duero, with an eleventh-century facade and arched windows, is traditionally known as the Casa del Cid.

Although the Parador stands on the site of a former Roman castle in the ancient precinct of the city, it is of much later construction and was built by the first Count of Alba and Aliste in 1459. The original building was much damaged during the uprising of the middle class *Comuneros* against the foreign entourage of the Emperor Charles V (see also page 148) and was reconstructed in Renaissance style by the fourth Count. The magnificent cloistered courtyard, as also the spacious glassed-in balcony above and the monumental stone staircase leading to it, date from this period. In 1798 the outer facade underwent extensive modification; and the building was used as an old people's home until it was acquired from the municipality by the M.I.T. As a footnote, the Parador possesses the largest bedroom of the whole chain, a vast suite, suitably equipped with a four-poster bed roomy enough for six.

Zamora is an historic city where one can pleasurably pass several days, and besides the Romanesque cathedral with its cupola in Byzantine style (marred by the pretentious seventeenth-century portal), it is remarkable for a multitude of churches, some dating from the twelfth century, and well worth visiting.

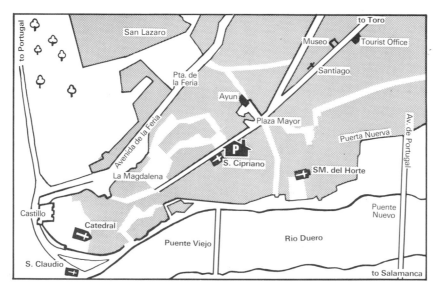

Above: Flying buttresses in a street in Zamora.

The fare, as the Spaniards say, is 'strong'. From the Parador's menu one may pick out *Chuleta de cerdo ahumada*, a most delicious form of pork chop, smoked exclusively in the village of Campofrío near Burgos; *Pierna de cabrito asada* (roast leg of kid); *Salteado de ternera 'toresana'* (a veal stew); *Magras de cerdo con tomate* (loin of pork in tomato sauce); *Sanantonada* (stewed haricot beans); and *Postre 'turco'* (a local variant of the ubiquitous caramel custard, served with cream).

The Province of Zamora, and in particular the vineyards around the ancient town of Toro, produce full bodied red wines, known locally as *Sangre de Toro* or bull's blood—to be confused neither with the Hungarian wine of the same name nor that from Villafranca del Panadés in Catalonia. Robust, deep in colour and sometimes containing as much as 13 or 14 per cent by volume of alcohol, these wines have always been favourites with the dons of Salamanca University and gave rise to the saying of one of the former rulers of León—Zamora forming part of the old kingship—*'Tengo un Toro que da vino y un León que se lo traga'* ('I have a Bull that gives wine and a Lion that swills it').

The Parador's carafe wine comes from Toro, and it also lists a rather more refined Tinto de Toro from the Bodegas Gato (of 13.8° strength). The best white wine of the region is from Rueda in the *Tierra del Vino* to the southeast. It is golden in colour, again strong in alcohol, and grows a *flor* in the manner of sherry; in flavour and bouquet it is not surprisingly reminiscent of Montilla, though lacking its finesse.

82

Right: The Renaissance court-yard of the Parador of the Condes de Alba y Aliste. Below: A doorway and rose window of the Cathedral of Zamora.

PIERNA DE CABRITO ASADA
ROAST LEG OF KID
Serves 6
Leg of kid or lamb
Salt
1 or 2 cloves of garlic
2oz (60gm) pork fat or olive oil
1 small glass of brandy
Put the meat in a baking tin, rub it with salt and garlic and moisten it with olive oil or daub it with pork fat. Preheat the oven and roast at moderate heat (375°F, Mark 5) for 20 minutes per pound. Half way through cooking add the brandy, which results in a golden colour and excellent flavour.

Remove the meat and place it on a dish in the oven to keep it hot. Skim off the fat from the juices in the roasting tin, add a little water and stir with a wooden spoon to mix with the juice, then pour this gravy over the roast before serving.

83

Until the twelfth century there was no distinction between Spain and Portugal; and both areas had been deeply penetrated by the Moors. It was the marriage of Count Henry of Burgundy to Teresa, an illegitimate daughter of Alfonso VI of León and Castile, and the conferment upon him in 1097 of the suzerainty of the lands between the Minho and Tagus rivers which began the separation. True to the family tradition, Henry's son, Afonso Henriques, squabbled bitterly with his cousin Alfonso VII, the new Emperor of Christian Spain, who insisted on regarding him as a vassal. The quarrel was complicated by the claims of another Burgundian, the Cluniac Bishop Gelmírez, for the supremacy of Santiago over the rival sees of Braga and Toledo. In the upshot, Afonso Henriques became de facto *King of Portugal by defeating the Moors at the Battle of Ourique and by his subsequent recapture of Lisbon and Evora and large tracts of territory to the south. His undisputed right to the title of King of Portugal was recognized by a bull promulgated by Pope Alexander III in 1179.*

Rey Fernando II de León: Benavente

Some years before this Papal bull Afonso had come to blows with Alfonso VII's successor, who built the castle that was to become the Parador of Fernando II de León at Benavente. During confused fighting in 1169 at Badajoz, which the Portuguese governor of Evora had seized from the Moors in violation of an agreement with Ferdinand, the besieging Portuguese were attacked from the rear by the Leonese and Afonso broke a leg and was captured.

Ferdinand II was constantly at war, either with the Moors, Castile or Portugal; he built the castle as a strongpoint near the Portuguese border, summoning a meeting of the Leonese Cortes (parliament) there in 1176. Henry of Trastámara (1369–79) gave it

Overleaf: The facade and gallery of the Parador of Rey Fernando II de Léon. Right: The keep.

to his natural son don Federico; and his grandson, Henry III (1390–1406), ceded it to the powerful family of Pimentel. During the Peninsular War, Napoleon planned to head off Sir John Moore's army at Benavente; and although Moore eluded him to begin the famous retreat to La Coruña, there was stiff fighting in the neighbourhood, during which the castle was heavily damaged by a French army under Marshal Lefebvre. It remained in a ruinous state until restored by the M.I.T.

Writing in 1502, Antoine de Lalaing, a French envoy to the court of the Catholic Monarchs (who stayed at the castle during a pilgrimage to Santiago de Compostela), describes its former glories: 'The Count [of Benavente] showed us his house from top to bottom. Inside, there are two galleries with richly carved and gilt ceilings; some of the pillars are of alabaster and others of marble, jasper and dressed stone. Adjoining, is a spacious hall, fifteen or sixteen feet wide and four hundred long, giving on to the river and the road to Galicia, and sumptuous to a degree; at the end, two elephantine pillars support an arch. We then saw eight or ten beautifully furnished rooms, whose ceilings were perfectly carved and gilt. I shall say nothing of the chapel; do not ask me if it is well-adorned; its vaulted roof soars higher than I can say and is so richly carved, gilt and painted that there is not another like it . . . In short, it is one of the most exquisite castles in Spain. The moat is flanked with stout towers, well-adapted for defence and provided with strong gates. . . .' De Lalaing adds that the garden was full of rare flowers and that the outlying park rang to the sound of the hunting horn, being well-stocked with hares (almost all white), camels, stags,

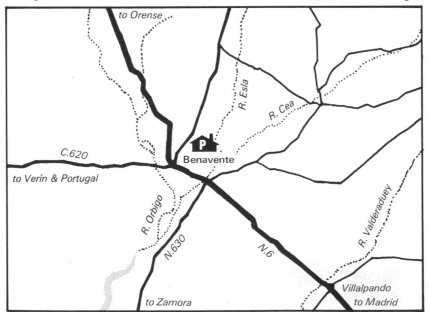

fallow deer, bucks, mountain goats—and even lions and leopards.

The castle was in large part built of brick, which as Federico Carlos Sainz de Robles wrote, 'has not been able to resist the ravages of time, of wars and of human neglect'; but both inside and in its great curtain walls and battlements much Gothic and Mudéjar work (the Mudéjars were Moors living in the reconquered areas) survives. The most impressive feature is the massive Renaissance keep, the so-called Torre del Caracol (Tower of the 'Snail'—a name given to the spiralling stone steps constructed for easy defence), built by Alonso de Pimentel, the fifth Count of Benavente, in the sixteenth century (the arms of the family are carved above the gates in the curtain wall). The interior has been carefully restored by M.I.T. and tastefully decorated, the large tapestries showing to advantage against the bare stonework of the walls.

Benavente is only some 70km north of Zamora, so that its regional specialities and wines are very much the same as those of the Parador of the Condes de Alba y Aliste, already described (see page 82). Its menu features *Bacalao a la tranca* (dried and salt cod) and *Presas de ternera* (veal), both cooked Zamoran style, and also *Rebozo zamorana*, a sponge cake with wine.

Some distance to the west at Verín and close to the northern border with Portugal is the modern Parador de Monterrey, built beneath the ruins of the mediaeval castle of the same name. The vineyards of Verín, in the sheltered valley of the River Támega, produce red wines of local repute and the strongest to come from Galicia: some contain up to 14° of alcohol. Typical of these are those from the Bodega Cooperativa de Monterrey, served at the Parador.

Below: Benavente was the scene of fierce fighting at the time of Sir John Moore's retreat to La Coruña during the Peninsular War. (The engraving by T. C. Stadler is from a contemporary watercolour by Sir Robert Kerr Porter.)

CACHELADA LEONESA
SPICED POTATOES FROM LEON
Serves 4
A warming winter dish from León, with a red and appetizing appearance. It is made with the local *chorizo*, a piquant sausage containing paprika, which comes in portions of about half a pound ($\frac{1}{4}$kg).
2lb (1kg) potatoes
2 *chorizos*, halved
Salt
Choose large, sound potatoes, peel them and cut into two or three. Put them in a pan with the *chorizo*, cover with water, season with salt and boil for 20 minutes. Pour off the water (which can be used for making soup) and serve the potatoes surrounded by the portions of *chorizo*.

BESUGO AL AJO ARRIERO
SEA BREAM COUNTRY STYLE
Serves 4
Fish
1 sea bream of about 2 to 3lb (1 to 1$\frac{1}{2}$kg)
Salt

1 onion, cut in half
Sprig of parsley
1 dessertspoon vinegar
Clean, wash and dry the sea bream, then put it in a fish pan or large
saucepan. Season with salt, add the onion, parsley and a little water,
and cook slowly for 20 minutes. It may alternatively be wrapped in
metal foil with the other ingredients and cooked for 20 minutes in a
moderate oven (350°F, Mark 4). Now place the fish on a heated serving
dish, reserving the stock, and keep hot while making the sauce.

Sauce
Olive oil
1 clove of garlic
1 teaspoon flour
1 teaspoon sweet paprika
1 teaspoon white vinegar
$\frac{1}{2}$ teacup fish stock
Heat a little olive oil in a saucepan and cook the garlic until golden,
then remove and discard it. Cook the flour in the oil, then stir in the
paprika powder, vinegar and fish stock. Check the seasoning and pour
the sauce over the bream. Serve with slices of lemon.

After the resounding Moorish defeat at Las Navas de Tolosa in 1212 neither side reacted with speed; and it was not until Ferdinand III had achieved the final union of León and Castile in 1230 that he was able to turn his full attention to the Reconquest of al-Andalus, capturing Córdoba, the ancient capital of the Caliphate in 1236. James the Conqueror of Aragon-Catalonia was similarly occupied with internal problems and it was not until 1238 that he recovered Valencia in the east. But the Christians were on the march; and only Ibn-al-Ahmar, the founder of the Nasrid dynasty of Granada, was to survive the onslaught.

In 1231 Ibn-al-Ahmar was just one of a number of Moorish chiefs fighting over the remains of the crumbling Almohad empire. From his base at Arjona near Córdoba, he soon made himself master of the surrounding area and about 1237 he captured Granada, occupying Málaga soon afterwards.

Castillo de Santa Catalina: Jaén

In 1245 Ibn-al-Ahmar's progress to the north was checked by the Castilians at Jaén, where he had built a fortress on the frowning hill above the city, now the site of the Parador of Santa Catalina. Deciding that discretion was the better part of valour, he ceded the castle and town to Ferdinand III and became his vassal in return for the control of Granada and the territory to the south. Ibn-al-Ahmar had to pay a stiff price by helping Ferdinand to subjugate the remainder of Andalusia. When, after assisting in the capture of Seville in 1248, he returned to Granada to be greeted with cries of 'Victor! Victor!', he replied with heavy heart, '*wa la ghaliba illa-llah*' ('There is no victor besides God'), a phrase which became the battle cry of the Nasrids and is repeatedly embodied in the decorative plaster work of the Alhambra, of which he laid the first foundations.

Although Ibn-al-Ahmar bought peace with the Christians at the expense of his compatriots, he used it to good effect to construct

The Parador of Santa Catalina with the towers of the Castle of Santa Catalina, from which it takes its name, in the background.

a chain of fortifications which were to ensure the survival of the Kingdom of Granada, alone among the Moorish emirates, for another two centuries.

After their occupation of Jaén, the Christians built a church beside the castle, dedicating it to St. Catherine. It is from this church, the ruins of which may still be seen, that the Parador takes its name. The Parador is not actually installed in the castle. To avoid disturbing the jagged silhouette, a landmark for miles around, M.I.T. has blasted the rock behind the Moorish ruin and constructed a building in relatively low profile, perching on the crag, with overhanging balconies, which is visible only from the approach road which winds round the steep hill. Clad in local stone, it harmonizes with the ruin; once inside, it would be difficult to guess that it is not an authentic mediaeval castle. Had Thurber's Walter Mitty been drawn to architecture, this might have been a favoured project!

Opposite: Scenes from an historical masque staged at the Parador of Santa Catalina. Below: An interior in the Parador.

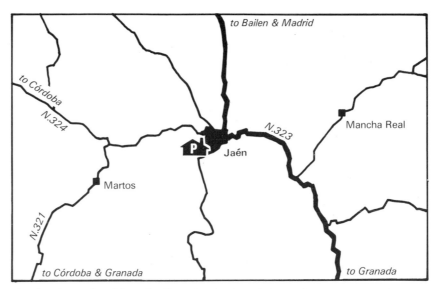

At the time of writing the Parador is closed for major reconstruction, so that it is not possible to give details of its menu. In its cooking, Jaén borrows something from the flamboyance of Andalusia, tempered by the more sober tastes of La Mancha. The three recipes that follow are typical of the region.

TERNERA CON ACEITUNAS
VEAL WITH OLIVES
Serves 4
2lb (1kg) fillet of veal
2oz (60gm) belly of pork, cut up
2 glasses dry white wine
Salt and pepper
1 dozen green olives
Put the veal in a roasting tin with the belly of pork on top, pour a glass of wine over it and season with salt and pepper. Preheat the oven and roast at moderate heat (375°F, Mark 5) for 1 hour. Check occasionally to make sure that it is not getting too dry; if it is, add a little water. When the meat is done, remove it and keep it hot, meanwhile pouring the other glass of wine into the juices in the roasting tin and stirring with a wooden spoon.

Cut the veal into thin slices, arrange on a serving dish, pour the sauce on top and garnish with the olives. This dish is best accompanied by artichoke hearts and new potatoes, boiled and garnished with butter and chopped parsley.

The following tomato sauce is served on the side.

SALSA DE TOMATE
TOMATO SAUCE
Olive oil
1 large onion, chopped
1lb (½kg) tomatoes, blanched, peeled and chopped, or a 1lb (½kg) tin of canned tomatoes
1 clove of garlic, squeezed

Opposite: Father Gonzalo de Illescas, one of the magnificent paintings commissioned from Zurbarán for the sacristy of the Monastery of Guadalupe.

95

1 small glass dry sherry
Salt and pepper
Heat the olive oil in a pan, fry the onion for 10 minutes and drain off
the oil. Add the tomatoes and garlic and cook for another 10 minutes
until the tomatoes are soft. Stir in the sherry, season with salt and
pepper, and then put into the blender or rub through a sieve.

PAVO A LA ANDALUZA
TURKEY ANDALUSIAN STYLE
Serves 6
1 turkey of about 6lb (3kg), cut up
2 onions, chopped
2 tomatoes, blanched, peeled and chopped
2 cloves of garlic, crushed
4 green pimientos, deseeded and cut up
Salt
1 bay leaf
1 clove
1 dessertspoon sweet paprika
1 large glass dry white wine
$\frac{1}{2}$ teaspoon olive oil
Put all the ingredients into a large stew pot, bring to the boil, then
reduce the heat, cover the pot, and simmer for about $2\frac{1}{2}$ to 3 hours or
until the turkey is tender. If necessary add a little water from time to
time—add only hot water, to avoid bringing the contents off the boil.

Opposite: The thirteenth-century castle built by Ibn-al-Ahmar of Granada and renamed Santa Catalina by the Christians.

Left: An interior in the Parador of Santa Catalina, which is a modern replica of a mediaeval castle.

96

With the final dissolution of the Almohad empire in North Africa in 1269, the Granadans looked for support to the new masters of Morocco, the Marinids, who responded by mounting a series of raids across the Strait of Gibraltar. Without posing any very serious threat to the Christians, these attacks diverted attention from Granada itself and allowed its rulers to consolidate their defences during a period when both Castile and Aragon were divided by quarrels over the succession, centring on the struggles of the Crown with the nobility.

The most menacing of the Marinid raids took place in 1340 when Abu 'l-Hasan, the sultan of Fez, crossed the Strait with a large army and laid siege to Algeciras. He was joined by Yusuf I of Granada, and the danger was such that Pope Benedict XII granted indulgence for a crusade. Alfonso XI of Castile was joined by strong forces under Afonso IV of Portugal. A battle took place near the mouth of the Salado river, and the Moors were decisively beaten. This was to be the last of the Berber invasions, which had begun six centuries before, though Gibraltar remained in Moorish hands until 1462.

Zurbarán: Guadalupe

It was in thanksgiving for his victory at Salado that Alfonso XI founded the Monastery of Nuestra Señora de Guadalupe, of which the building now occupied by the Parador of Zurbarán was once a dependence.

The legend of the Virgin of Guadalupe goes back to the first years of the Moorish invasion in 711. At that time, some fugitive monks from Seville buried a wooden image of the Virgin in the locality. It was unearthed towards the end of the thirteenth century by a shepherd from Cáceres, Gil Cordero, and miraculously found to be undamaged. A small hermitage was built to accommodate it

Guadalupe and its monastery.

and it soon became the object of a pilgrimage, because of the many favours and miracles granted by the Virgin.

In 1389 the monastery was entrusted to the Hieronymites (or Order of St. Jerome), and Prior Fernando Yáñez much embellished the building, adding a splendid Mudéjar cloister and the superb library and chapter house. In its mountain fastness on the eastern border of the Extremadura, the shrine now became almost as famous as Santiago de Compostela. Much frequented by the Catholic Monarchs, it was here that they signed the documents authorizing Columbus's first voyage to America; and the Island of Guadalupe, discovered on his second voyage, was named after it. The Virgin of Guadalupe became the patron of the *Conquistadores*; and Richard Ford, as staunchly Protestant as his contemporary George Borrow, notes that, 'Cortés, on landing in Spain, in 1583, hurried to worship her image for nine days. He and his followers hoped by offering at her altar the *spolia optima* of their strangely achieved wealth, to obtain death-bed pardons.'

Not only the *Conquistadores*, but also generations of princes and grandees of Spain enriched the monastery, so that at the time when it was sacked by the French during the Peninsular War it was a veritable storehouse of treasures. A great deal remains today. The little wooden image of the Virgin, blackened by the kisses of countless pilgrims, still stands in a small chamber high above the main altar. Other treasures include one of the most extensive collections in the world of jewelled tapestries and surplices and a remarkable series of illuminated chorals. In 1638 Zurbarán arrived at the monastery to paint what is perhaps his finest work, the Apotheosis, and the eight famous canvasses of scenes from the life of St. Jerome, which line the walls of the sacristary.

Above: One of the many illuminated chorus books preserved at the Monastery of Guadalupe.

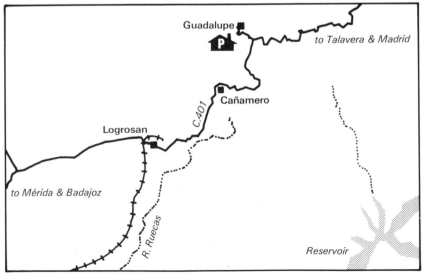

Above: A wooden effigy of the Virgin of Guadalupe, the patron saint of the Conquistadors, which was unearthed in the thirteenth century.

Below: The Parador of Zurbarán from the garden.

The Parador, named after Zurbarán, is housed, appropriately enough, in the old Colegio de los Infantes and Hospital de San Juan Bautista, built in the fifteenth century as hospices for the pilgrims. The frontage is continuous and gives on to the monastery, so that it is only a step down the hilly street to the great flight of steps leading up to its entrance. The stern facade of the Parador hides a charming arcaded patio with access to the main rooms, which have been altered as little as possible. The bedrooms to the rear open out on to balconies overlooking a garden in Moorish style, with fountains and irrigation channels and a swimming pool in a corner. Its grey-green olive trees produce a crop which is not edible without the usual long process of marination; but hidden by the garage below are two spreading fig trees whose fruit is as luscious as it looks.

Among the typical Extremenian dishes served by the Parador are *Gazpacho extremeño*, a cold soup containing hard-boiled egg, tomatoes, garlic, olive oil, almonds, salt and vinegar; *Trucha frita a la extremeña* (fried trout, Extremenian style); *Carbonada guadalupense* (veal grilled over charcoal); *Lomo de cerdo mudéjar* (loin of pork); and *Muegado de Guadalupe*, a sweet made by frying a paste of flour and egg with honey.

The neighbouring village of Cañamero makes a distinctive wine, available at the bars in Guadalupe or in carafes at the Parador. It is orange in colour and slightly turbid, with a pronounced flavour of sherry. Like the wines from Rueda and Montánchez (see pages 82 and 44), it grows a *flor*. For people interested in such things, it is worth stopping off at Cañamero on the way up to Guadalupe from the south and visiting one of the bodegas where it is made. During fermentation in large earthenware jars, the must looks like muddy, bubbling water; and the protective film of yeast on top can clearly be seen.

ALCACHOFAS SALTEADAS CON JAMON
GLOBE ARTICHOKES WITH HAM
Serves 2 as a starter
8oz (225gm) tin of artichoke hearts
1oz (30gm) butter
2oz (60gm) cooked ham, chopped
1 onion, chopped
A little chopped parsley
Salt and pepper
Drain the artichokes and reserve. Heat the butter in a pan and fry the ham and onion; when the onion is golden, add the artichoke hearts, stir well and continue cooking for 2 or 3 minutes, sprinkling in the parsley, salt and pepper at the last moment. Serve piping hot.

HUEVOS A LA EXTREMADURA
EGGS FROM THE EXTREMADURA
Serves 4
Olive oil
1 onion, finely chopped
2 tomatoes, blanched, peeled and cut up

1lb ($\frac{1}{2}$kg) potatoes, boiled and cut up
5oz (150gm) *chorizo*, sliced
5oz (150gm) cooked ham, cut up
Salt and pepper
4 eggs
7oz (200gm) cooked garden peas

Heat a little olive oil in a pan and fry the onion for 10 minutes, then remove it with a draining spoon and pour off and reserve the oil. Return the onion to the pan, add the tomatoes and cook together for 5 minutes. Now add the potatoes, *chorizo*, ham and a little salt and pepper, and cook for a further 15 minutes.

Transfer to an oven dish and break the eggs over the mixture, garnishing with the peas. Bake in a hot oven until the whites are set, the yolks remaining soft.

Below: A reception room in the Parador of Zurbarán.

Above: The courtyard of the
Parador of La Concordia, part
of which dates from the thirteenth century. Right: An abandoned monastery in the wild
mountain region of the Maestrazgo bordering Alcañiz.
Overleaf: A distant view of the
Parador of La Concordia, sur-
mounting the hill above the
town of Alcañiz.

If Wilfred the Hairy was the founder of an independent Catalonia, it was his descendant Ramón Berenguer IV who, by marrying the Infanta Petronila of neighbouring Aragon in 1137 and uniting the two kingdoms in the teeth of opposition from Castile, put Aragon-Catalonia on the high road to fame and fortune. During the next three centuries the Crown of Aragon, as it was thenceforth known, was to become one of the most powerful maritime and trading nations of the Mediterranean, rivalling Genoa and Venice. On the mainland its rulers held sway over the coastal area from Alicante in the south to the Roussillon and Provence in the north; and further afield the Catalans occupied the Balearics, Sicily, Sardinia, Corsica, the Kingdom of Naples and even a region in Greece.

This expansion was achieved on a sound economic basis. Successive Castilian monarchs had made over to the nobility from the north the territories recaptured from the Moors. The hard-working Moorish peasants or skilled Mudéjar artisans were forced out; the empty lands were repopulated by sheep; and the Castilian economy became virtually dependent on the Mesta, *an organization of large landowners which in 1237 was granted a monopoly of the wool trade with Flanders and Italy. James the Conqueror of Catalonia pursued a much more liberal and diversified policy, settling farmers on smaller plots of land, making use of Mudéjar skills, and encouraging the growth of a mercantile middle class. Hand in hand with economic progress and military and commercial expansion overseas went a healthy respect for individual liberties; and the* Usatges, *or code of civil rights, was promulgated a century and a half before the* Magna Carta.

The development of the Crown of Aragon was viewed somewhat jealously from Castile; and though the two states were united in the cause of Reconquest, there had been constant bickering over the redivision of the recaptured Moorish territories on their borders. When the dynasty of the Counts of Barcelona came to an end with the death of Martin I in 1410, the appearance of the Castilian Ferdinand of Antequera as a candidate for the throne caused immediate dissension, since the Catalans feared—not without reason, as subsequent events were to prove—that their kingdom would increasingly fall within the orbit of Castile.

La Concordia: Alcañiz

It was at the Castle of Alcañiz, now the Parador of La Concordia, that the Aragonese Parliament met in 1412 to decide on steps that were to lead to Ferdinand's triumph over his Catalan rival, Count James of Urgel. Ferdinand was a grandson of Henry II of Castile, the bastard brother of Pedro the Cruel, who by rebelling against him and finally murdering him in 1369 had established the Trastámara dynasty that was to rule Castile and Aragon until the death of Ferdinand the Catholic in 1516. Although stubbornly opposed by the Catalans, Ferdinand had powerful allies in Aragon and in the shape of the evangelizing St. Vincente Ferrer and the Anti-pope Pedro de Luna, representing the Church. A loaded Parliament referred the issue to a further commission held at Caspe later the same year, at which Ferdinand was duly elected. The unfortunate Count James was captured and lived out the rest of his days in a subterranean dungeon at Játiva. These events are (somewhat euphemistically) recorded by a plaque on the main stairway of the Parador.

The castle, roughly half way between Saragossa and Tarragona, tops the steep hill and precipitous streets of the surrounding town, and is visible for miles around. Its elegant eighteenth-century facade, constructed by the Infante don Philip in 1728, belies the age of the building. It was ceded to the Order of Calatrava (formed like the Knights Templars to fight against the Saracens) by Alfonso II of Aragon in 1179. Much of the older part, to the rear of don Philip's palace now used as the Parador, dates from the thirteenth century. The ruined Romanesque chapel communicates with a

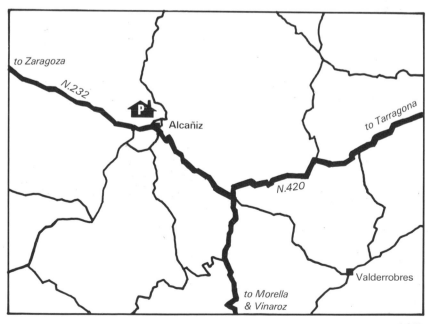

Opposite: A reception room in the Parador of La Concordia.

chapter house, where, in the romantic words of one of its Spanish historians, 'under the insignia of their order and in front of an altar bare except for the two ritual candles, the warlike Masters of Calatrava, with an itch for power and a talent for intrigue, voiced their quarrels, staked out claims to lands, licensed concessions, declared war and entered into alliances. Their badges glowed in the candle-light, which glinted from the swords so out of keeping with a house of religion.' This chapter house was also the venue of a more peaceful meeting in 1372 when Henry of Trastámara and Pedro the Ceremonious of Aragon agreed to submit their differences to the Pope. In latter years the castle also played a part in the Napoleonic and Carlist Wars.

The infant Ferdinand of Antequera, for whose accession to the Crown of Aragon the Aragonese Parliament declared in 1412 at the Castle of Alcañiz. (From a painting by an anonymous Spanish artist.)

The dining room, vast in scale like the other rooms of the eighteenth-century palace, is lined with tapestries depicting the arms of successive Masters of Calatrava and other illustrious chatelaines. In culinary terms Aragon and Navarre are known as the *Zona de los Chilindrónes*—piquant sauces containing onions, peppers and tomatoes; and this is the place to try *Pollo a la chilindrón* (chicken in Chilindrón sauce). Other specialities are: *Sopa de Teruel en perolico*, a soup served from a small kettle; *Menestra de verduras Concordia*, a vegetable stew; *Ternasco asado*, roast lamb; *Lomo de cerdo aragonesa*, fillet of pork; *Conejo escabechado tirolense*, marinated rabbit; and *Tortas de alma*, a sweet made from a cake typical of Alcañiz. The region is famous for the quality of its olive oil, and the menu carries a note stating that the oil used in the kitchens is guaranteed by the Sindicato Nacional del Olivo.

Although not itself in a wine-growing area, Alcañiz is close both to Tudela in Navarre and Cariñena in the Province of Saragossa, both of which produce wines of repute. Tudela, on the Ebro, makes robust wines of 15° to 17° strength; the cooperative-made wines of Cariñena, again strong in alcohol, are sold all over Spain for everyday drinking.

To the south of Alcañiz, the modern Parador of Teruel, in a town famous both for its role in the Civil War and for the Legend of its Lovers, has always enjoyed a good reputation for its cooking, which is also Aragonese in style.

POLLO A LA CHILINDRON
CHICKEN IN CHILINDRON SAUCE
Serves 4
Olive oil
Pork fat
1 chicken of about 4lb (2kg), cut up
1 onion, chopped
2 cloves of garlic, squeezed
5 canned red peppers, cut up
Salt and pepper
Heat some mixed pork fat and olive oil in a pan and fry the pieces of chicken over a high flame until browned. Transfer to a stew pot and add the tomatoes, onion, garlic and strips of red pepper, and season with salt and pepper. The tomatoes and peppers will provide enough water for slow cooking, which should be continued for about 1 hour or until the chicken is tender. If it is a bit dry, add a little white wine and water.

TERNASCO ASADO
ROAST LEG OF LAMB
Serves 4
3lb (1½kg) leg of lamb or other cut, in one piece
Salt
7oz (200gm) pork fat
Juice of 2 lemons
1 glass dry white wine
Place the joint in a roasting tin, cover with the pork fat, season with salt and moisten with the lemon juice and white wine. Roast in a moderately hot oven (375°F, Mark 5) for 20 minutes per pound (½kg), basting from time to time.

109

The small Basque Kingdom of Navarre sprang up around what was its only large town in mediaeval times, Pamplona. After the expulsion of the Moors, the most powerful of its early rulers was Sancho the Great, who by his death in 1035 had amalgamated it with Castile and occupied most of León. This period of expansion was short-lived and it was soon afterwards partitioned between Alfonso VI of Castile and Sancho Ramírez of Aragon. Reconstituted in 1134, it came under French domination a century later, but recovered its independence in 1328. Hemmed in as it was by Castile, Aragon and France, and so denied the opportunity to extend its territory at the expense of the Moors during the Reconquest, it remained a bone of contention between its more powerful neighbours. By exploiting their differences, Charles II (1349–87) gained Navarre a further respite.

Príncipe de Viana: Olite

It was his son, Charles III ('The Noble'), who built the Castle of Olite, which has taken on a new lease of life as the Parador of the Príncipe de Viana. Olite, 40 kilometres south of Pamplona, had been a favourite residence of the kings of Navarre since the twelfth century, and when Charles began the work of construction about 1403 it was on the site of a much earlier building. When finished in 1413, it was the largest and most elaborate fortified palace in Spain, and it is said that it possessed one room for every day of the year. Pedro de Madrazo, the Navarrese historian, has written: 'At that

The Parador of the Príncipe de Viana viewed from the Church of Santa Maria la Real.

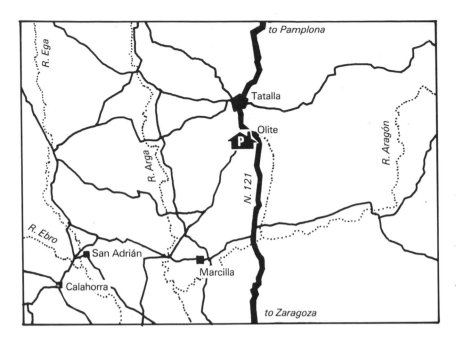

time Navarre, more than any other kingdom, excited the greed
of the kings and barons of the neighbouring countries; and for
that reason its kings, always on their guard, habitually resorted
to subterranean passages, watch towers, galleries with hidden
exits, spiral staircases and secret doors, as a guarantee of security.
From the outside, the defensive works therefore looked irregular
and haphazard. All the walls were battlemented and machicolated;
and at the many salients, asymmetrical and of differing heights,
small cylindrical towers were built out on projecting corbals. Two
strikingly contrasted colours predominate: the red of the sandstone
walls and the white of the limestone and marble used for interior
galleries, columns and keystoned windows. To the east is a solitary
watch tower, joined to the castle proper by a bridge . . .'

Of the original fifteen towers, only three—those of *Las Atalayas*
('The Look-outs'), *Los Cuatro Vientos* ('The Four Winds') and
Las Tres Coronas ('The Three Crowns')—now remain. But since
the reconstruction by M.I.T. one can no longer say, as did Juan
Iturralde, that 'past clamour has given way to a sepulchral silence,
interrupted only by the noise of a falling stone, consigning to
limbo one more letter from the Book of History.' The interior has
been carefully restored and suitably furnished: some of the bedrooms have been equipped with four-posters; and, as always in
such establishments, one must be prepared for the knight in armour
or chainmail in an angle of the stairs! Across the stone-flagged
square and connected with the castle by a subterranean passage is
the Church of Santa María la Real, with its twelfth-century tower

and beautiful Romanesque entrance.

It was in this castle that Charles the Noble convened the Parliament of Navarre in 1410, 1413, and in 1419 to make arrangements for the marriage of his daughter, Blanca, to John II of Aragon. The fruit of this marriage was Charles, Prince of Viana, who spent his childhood at Olite and from whom the Parador has taken its name. His unjust exclusion from the succession by his father, with whom he spent his life in bitter conflict, engendered a civil war between the rival factions of the *Agramonteses* and *Beaumonteses*, representing the two most powerful families of Navarre. The Prince of Viana aspired to the hand of Isabel of Castile, but his father had other plans and arranged for her betrothal to Ferdinand, a son by his second marriage. A popular favourite, whose remains were afterwards hallowed as those of a saint, the Prince of Viana died young in 1479; and the marriage between Ferdinand and Isabel, consummated some years before, led to the union of Castile and Aragon. Ironically enough, Ferdinand was to invade Navarre in 1512, to overwhelm the Castle of Olite, and to put an end to the kingdom's existence as an independent state. Spanish Navarre was incorporated in Castile and its territories beyond the Pyrenees ceded to France.

Much later, in 1813, the castle, which had fallen into disrepair, was burnt at the orders of the guerrilla leader, General Mina, to prevent its falling into the hands of the French. As a somewhat bizarre footnote, Olite played its part in the development of the national sport of bull-fighting. A document of 1387, preserved in the city archives, records that Charles III ordered 90 *libras* to be paid to three *matatoros* from Saragossa for fighting a number of 'brave bulls' in the courtyard of the castle.

Right: The model winery of the Señorio de Sarría near Olite, which produces some of the best Navarre wine.

The menu lists some specialities from Navarre, such as *Menestra de Tudela*, a vegetable stew; *Cordero en chilindrón*, lamb in Chilindrón sauce (see page 109); and *Costillas de cordero a la parilla*, charmingly translated as 'Mutton Cuttles'. There are also some sweets typical of nearby Pamplona and Estella.

The most interesting of the Parador's regional wines are those from the Señorio de Sarría, an estate situated near Puente de la Reina, on the old pilgrim route to Santiago de Compostela, and south of Pamplona. Although Navarre has long been noted for its wines, production at the Señorio began only in 1952. It is a model estate, also incorporating gardens, orchards and a stock-raising establishment; and the bodega was begun as the caprice of a wealthy industrialist. But there is nothing amateurish about the wines, which are made from carefully selected varieties of grape grown on the domaine and aged in oak barrels newly bought each year—in this respect Chateau Mouton Rothschild and H. Beaumont & Co. of the Señorio de Sarría must be unique. All the wines, white, rosé and red are of high quality—from the inexpensive three-year-old Ecoyen to the magnificent Gran Reserva of 1964, a beautiful wine, fruity and well-bodied with a fine bouquet. The Señorio is not alone in making good wine, and those from the Viñícola Navarra, adjoining it at Las Campanas, are also of good quality.

114

HUEVOS AL PLATO A LA NAVARRA
EGGS NAVARRE STYLE
Serves 4
8 eggs
A little butter or olive oil
4 tomatoes, fried
Salt and pepper
A little chopped parsley
8 slices *chorizo de Pamplona*, fried
2oz (60gm) grated cheese
Heat a little butter or olive oil in individual *cazuelas* or small fireproof casseroles. Divide up the fried tomato between the *cazuelas* and sprinkle with the chopped parsley and a little salt and pepper. Break the eggs on top and arrange the slices of cooked *chorizo* around the sides, sprinkling them with the grated cheese. The *cazuelas* may now be put into the oven or cooking may be finished over a low flame, so as to set the whites while leaving the yolks soft.

The Parador of the Príncipe de Viana, former palace and stronghold of the Kings of Navarre.

115

Left: A hall in the Parador of the Príncipe de Viana. Below: The Church of Santa María la Real, connected to the castle by an underground passage.

Cavalier, the country is a horrible one, say nothing to the contrary. We are all frightened, the young ladies, the young gentleman, and myself; even his worship is frightened, and says we are come to this country for our sins. It rains every day, and this is almost the first time that we have seen the sun since our arrival. It rains continually, and one cannot step out without being up to the ancles in fango . . .

The quotation is from The Bible in Spain *by George Borrow; the lament is not George Borrow's, but that of an Andalusian maidservant of the ex-Receiver General of Granada, exiled to Galicia after a shake-up in his Ministry. And yet . . . from mid-May to mid-September the little-explored mountains of Galicia are an endless rock garden, riotous with flowers and heavy with the fragrance of pine and eucalyptus. Add to this the secluded beaches washed by the Atlantic, the fresh and lively wines and a cuisine as various as any in Spain, and Galicia seems a part of the world undeservedly neglected by tourists from abroad.*

Condes de Villalba: Villalba

The Parador of the Condes de Villalba, installed in a fortress dating from about the same period as Olite, cannot be directly related to the mainstream of Spanish history, but is well worth a visit. The little town of Villalba in the extreme northwest of the country is off the main road from Lugo to La Coruña. The great octagonal Torre de los Andrade is one of the best examples of a fourteenth-century Galician keep. In a state bordering on collapse when it was taken in hand by M.I.T., the exterior has been meticulously restored and the inside entirely reconstructed. The approach is by a wooden bridge; a lift and six large double bedrooms occupy the upper part of the tower; and a lofty raftered dining room has been installed below the level of the entrance.

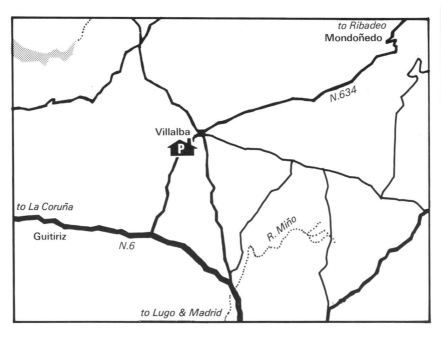

Above: The Castle of Villalba, after its reconstruction as a Parador.

As Borrow noted, Galicia can be one of the wettest and coldest parts of Spain—witness the deprivations of Sir John Moore's troops during the calvary of their retreat to La Coruña—and the Parador's menu is a first-rate compendium of the robust and heartening local fare.

All of its sixteen regional specialities are well-prepared and appetizing—but the quantities are so generous that it is as well to share portions if one wants to sample more than a couple. A good start is the *Caldo o crema a la gallega*; described in the colourful menu notes as containing 'flowers and green turnisps, grease, potatoes, white beans and sausage', this is in fact an excellent Galician version of the Portuguese *Caldo Verde*, the 'flowers and green turnisps' referring to the sprouting tops of the vegetable, known in Portugal as *grelos*. The *Empanada gallega* should on no account be missed; it is a thick tart

118

filled with onions, tomatoes and peppers, together with either sardines or loin of pork.

Villalba is not far from the coast, and the fish is excellent. *Caldeirada gallega* is a dish akin to the French bouillabaisse, and very like the Portuguese fish stews of the same name. The *Conchas de peregrino* could again be compared to *Coquilles St. Jacques*: the scallops are served in their shells with a little garlic, onion and parsley and browned with breadcrumbs. The *Calamares rellenos* (stuffed inkfish) and *Pulpo a feira*, octopus spiced with red peppers, are recommended to those who like such strong fare.

At this point most diners will call it a day; but the Parador also offers some satisfying meat dishes, such as *Lacón con grelos*, ham bone with *chorizo* and sprouting turnip tops; and *Callos a la gallega*, a revelation to those accustomed only to the bland English tripe and onions, and more in the style of the famous *Tripas à modo do Porto*. Whatever you choose, leave room for the *Filloas*, cream-filled pancakes cooked in liqueur.

The Galician cuisine is not for slimmers, but is one of the most varied in Spain; simpler consommés, omelettes and grills are also, of course, available.

This northernmost tip of the country produces no wine. The Parador nevertheless lists various 'green wines' from further south in Galicia (see page 193), including the excellent dry white Albariño from Fefiñanes, together with a selection of Riojas and a very drinkable *vino común* (*vin ordinaire*) in carafes.

EMPANADA GALLEGA
This savoury tart may be made with a variety of fillings—either meat or fish, often fresh sardines—but always contains *chorizo*, tomatoes and peppers.
Pastry
1lb 2oz (500gm) flour, sieved
1 egg yolk
2½oz (75gm) pork fat
⅙oz (5gm) yeast powder
Heap the flour on a marble slab or pastry board, make a hole in the top and add the other ingredients, then moisten with enough tepid water for the paste to come away from your hands and the board. Knead thoroughly as if making bread, cover with a cloth and leave for about 1 hour until cracks appear in the dough. Now resume thorough working of the dough with your hands and roll it out. Grease a large tart tin and cut two circles of dough, one to line the tin and the other to place on top of the filling. Keep any trimmings to seal the top at the last moment.

Filling
Olive oil
1 large onion, chopped
1lb (½kg) tomatoes, blanched, peeled and cut up
1 bay leaf
Salt and pepper
Parsley
½lb (250gm) cooked chicken, minced

½lb (250gm) loin of pork, cut up and fried
3oz (90gm) *chorizo*, thinly sliced
4 canned red peppers, cut into strips
1 egg, beaten

Heat some olive oil in a pan, fry the onion for 5 minutes, drain off excess oil and add the garlic, tomatoes, bay leaf, parsley and a little salt and pepper. Cook slowly for 5 minutes, then stir in the chicken, pork, *chorizo* and peppers. Simmer for 15 minutes to make a smooth mixture and allow to cool.

Fill the lined tart tin with this mixture, seal with the second circle of pastry and make a small hole at the centre. Brush the pastry with beaten egg. Meanwhile heat the oven to 425°F (Mark 7) for 20 minutes. Turn down to moderate heat (375°F, Mark 5) and bake for about ½ hour or 45 minutes until the top of the tart is crisp and golden.

Another good filling may be made by substituting ½ pound (250gm) each of cooked, chopped ham and smoked haddock, boiled, skinned and boned, in place of the pork and chicken.

FILLOAS

These pancakes, which are rather thicker than is usual in Britain, are filled with jam or compote of fruit, rolled over and sprinkled with castor sugar before serving.

To make 6 pancakes
4oz (110gm) flour
Pinch of salt
1 egg
½ pint (3dl) milk

Sieve the flour and salt into a basin, make a well in the middle and drop in an egg. Stir with a wooden spoon, gradually adding ¼ pint (1½dl) milk and using all the flour to make a smooth batter.

Beat with a whisk to remove lumps and then incorporate the rest of the milk. Allow to rest for 20 minutes.

Now grease a small omelette pan (7½in or 19cm) and heat until it begins to smoke. Add 3 or 4 tablespoons of the batter and shake the pan so that it spreads out evenly. Cook quickly until the pancake is golden underneath and bubbly on top. Slide in a palette knife, turn over and cook on the other side.

The Castle of Villalba, before its reconstruction as a parador.

Even at its peak Nasrid Granada was small, comprising a narrow coastal strip extending from Gibraltar in the south to the region between Almería and Cartagena in the north. Into this small area there crowded great numbers of Moorish refugees from the territories reoccupied by the Christians. Thanks to their industry and skill, the kingdom prospered and the city of Granada became a byword for its riches and douceur de vivre, *symbolized by the palace of the Alhambra and the hanging gardens of the Generalife, perhaps the most successful fusion of architecture and landscape achieved by man.*

For more than two centuries from its formation by Ibn-al-Ahmar in 1237 its rulers warded off the Christian Reconquest, at times by paying tribute and at others by a tenacious defence of their mountain boundaries. But the position had changed since Christian, Saracen and Jew could live peacefully together, as they had done in the past. Economic rivalry manifested itself in religious conflict, of which the Jews were the first victims; and when Christian Spain adopted a belief in the identity of the state and a single religion, peaceful co-existence was no longer possible. Once Castile and the Crown of Aragon had been united under the Catholic Monarchs, Isabel and Ferdinand, in 1479, the survival of a Muslim enclave in a Greater Spain became increasingly less acceptable.

Ferdinand and Isabel made concerted plans for the overthrow of the emirate; the Pope declared a crusade; and, ironically enough with Jewish finance, they were able to equip a powerful army. The first Christian successes were in the south of the kingdom; and after capturing the outlying mountain bastion of Ronda in 1485, Ferdinand moved in on the great city of Málaga in 1487.

Gibralfaro: Málaga

The key to Málaga's defences was the great Moorish citadel on a hill dominating the city and port, which has given its name to the Parador of Gibralfaro, facing the ruins of the castle. Ferdinand offered an honourable capitulation to the inhabitants, which they would have accepted but for the presence of the numerous Christian renegades in the city and the fierce resistance of a group of Berbers driven from Ronda, who had seized the fortress. During the ensuing siege of forty days the King lost 100 knights and 200 foot soldiers. Having gone to such trouble to reduce the place, Ferdinand now refused any terms except unconditional surrender when the starving inhabitants finally treated with him. In the event, he decided to make an example of Málaga to the towns in the Kingdom which still held out. Its citizens were deported *en masse* to other parts of Spain and those unable to pay crippling ransoms were sold into slavery. It was to celebrate his victory that Ferdinand granted the new Christian city of Málaga arms which display the silhouette of Gibralfaro on a heraldic ground.

Above: The Christians attack a Moorish citadel (wood carving from the Choir of Toledo Cathedral).

The castle was built about 787—perhaps on a Phoenician or Greek site—by 'Abd-al-Rahman I, the first of the Umayyad emirs of Córdoba, and was called Djabal Faro ('the hill of light') by the Muslims, because of a great beacon on one of its towers, which lit up marauding pirate vessels and guided home lost merchantmen. The fortifications were much extended during the reign of 'Abd-al-Rahman III in the tenth century, when a great cistern, 38 metres deep and capable of supplying water for a garrison of 5,000, was cut into the living rock.

The fortress was virtually impregnable—as emerges from the picturesque legend of the Carrier Pigeon of Gibralfaro. During the period of the Party Kings in the eleventh century, Málaga owed allegiance to Badis ibn-Habus of Granada, but was much coveted by the powerful al-Mu'tadid, emir of Seville. Entering into a conspiracy with Badis's disaffected subjects in Málaga, al-Mu'tadid despatched an expedition under his son, Muhammad. The city fell without a struggle; but a party loyal to Badis took refuge in Gibralfaro and, refusing all demands to surrender, sent a carrier pigeon to Granada with a plea for help. Badis at once mobilized his army and fell upon the unsuspecting Muhammad, who, according to the legend (and in breach of the injunctions of the Koran) had surrendered himself to women and wine. The rout was complete; and Muhammad escaped only by dressing in women's clothes and riding over the mountains to Ronda. This inglorious episode can hardly have endeared him to his masterful father, who

122

later had him put to death on suspicion of treachery.

The Parador, which is approached from the city by a steep, winding road, was first built by M.I.T. as an *hostería*, but has more recently been extended, with the provision of hotel facilities. There are beautiful views of the castle and a wide panorama of the smiling blue bay from its arcaded terraces, which are a delightful spot for an *al fresco* lunch or dinner.

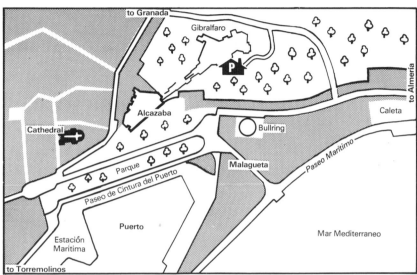

Below: Part of the modern Parador of Gibralfaro.

During its days as an hostería and in territory not always remarkable for the quality of its beef, the restaurant served first-rate steak *aux poivres*. Long may the tradition continue; but more typical of the region are *Sopa de uvas blancas malagueña*, a cold soup made with grapes and almonds and most refreshing on a hot day; *Sopa de pescado malagueña*, a broth containing a variety of different fish; and *Fritura mixta de pescados* (mixed fried fish, see page 130). The neighbouring shores abound in fish; and particularly delicious are the tiny *Chanquetes*, either fried crisp like whitebait or made into an omelette (*Tortilla de chanquetes*). The shellfish is also plentiful and to be recommended; and here or elsewhere in Andalusia one should try *Huevos a la flamenca* (see page 124). There are various local sweets, such as *Dulce malagueño* (made with semolina, egg yolks, sponge fingers, raisins and quince compote); but perhaps the best dessert on a hot day is fresh fruit or the *Tarta helada* (iced cake), served at most of the Paradores up and down the country.

The sweet fortified wines of Málaga have been famous since Roman days and are made from Moscatel and Pedro Ximénez grapes grown in the hills behind the city—hence the old name of 'Mountain Wine'. With the current fashion for dry wines their popularity has declined; but if your taste is for a good dessert wine, this is the opportunity to indulge it. The best-known of the producers are Scholtz Hermanos.

During the meal, especially when eating fish, a good choice of wine is dry Montilla, a sherry-like but unfortified wine made near Córdoba, which should be drunk chilled.

123

AJO BLANCO CON UVAS DE MALAGA
COLD GARLIC SOUP WITH GRAPES
Serves 4
20 almonds, blanched
4 cloves of garlic, peeled
1 teaspoon salt
2oz (60gm) toasted breadcrumbs, soaked and drained
4 dessertspoons refined olive oil
2 dessertspoons vinegar
7oz (200gm) white grapes, skinned and without pips
Grind the almonds, garlic and salt in a mortar, add the moist breadcrumbs and continue until a smooth paste is obtained. Transfer this to a large bowl and drip in the olive oil, at the same time stirring with a wooden spoon as if making a mayonnaise. Incorporate the vinegar in the same way. Now pour in $1\frac{1}{4}$ pints ($\frac{3}{4}$ litre) of cold water, stirring well with the spoon. Check the seasoning and finally add the grapes. Serve chilled.

HUEVOS A LA FLAMENCA
EGGS FLAMENCA
Serves 2
2 onions, sliced
Olive oil
4oz (110gm) bacon, chopped
2 or 3 tomatoes, blanched, peeled and sliced
Salt and pepper
1 or 2 eggs per person
4oz (110gm) peeled prawns (fresh, or frozen and defrosted)
4oz (110gm) *chorizo*, sliced
1 small can red peppers, cut into strips
Fry the onions in olive oil until tender. Drain off the oil, add the bacon and tomatoes and continue frying for another 5 to 10 minutes. Season to taste. Remove the mixture with a draining spoon and divide it between 2 small *cazuelas* or individual casseroles. Place the slices of *chorizo* around the edges of the dishes, then break the eggs into the middle and cook rapidly on top of the stove so that the whites are set and the yolks soft. At the last moment add the prawns and decorate the top with the strips of red pepper.

Opposite: The Alhambra, Court of the Myrtles.

Left: An *horreo*, typical of Galicia and built on stilts to store grain away from rats. Below: After a night at sea, a fisherman plucks his catch from the nets.

126

While the rulers of Granada were split by a bitter family feud, Ferdinand moved in relentlessly on the city itself. By 1491 he had invaded its luxuriant vega *with an army of 40,000 foot soldiers and 10,000 cavalry and established a tented encampment nearby at Santa Fe. The last and luckless Muslim king, Boabdil, who had previously been engaged in devious negotiations with Ferdinand, now decided to hold out to the end.*

Queen Isabel, who had accompanied her husband on the expedition and came near to losing her life when her tent caught fire in a blaze that swept the camp, was equally determined and made a vow to found a Franciscan monastery within the enclave of the Alhambra on the fall of the city. In November 1491 Boabdil treated for surrender and on 2 January 1492, he delivered over the keys of the Alhambra before riding off into oblivion, pursued by his mother's ringing epitaph: 'Weep like a woman for what you could not defend like a man.'

San Francisco: Granada

Isabel kept her vow and duly founded the monastery, now the Parador of San Francisco. It was built on the site of an old mosque and palace, reconstructed between 1333 and 1354 by Yusuf I, perhaps the greatest of the Nasrid emirs. The chapel at the centre incorporates some of the beautiful arches and intricately figured plasterwork of the original building; and it was here that Isabel and Ferdinand were interred before the removal of their bodies to Granada Cathedral on its completion in 1521.

The monastery was reconstructed in 1545 and again in 1729 and fell into disrepair after the expropriation of the monks in 1835. Thereafter it was used as a barracks, a storehouse and an old people's home, until it was restored by the Ministry of Fine Arts between 1927 and 1929 and reopened as an art school. The Dirección General de Turismo began its conversion to a Parador in 1944, separating the chapel and former tomb of the Catholic Monarchs from the rest of the building. Some of the original work remains, notably a square room with Mozarabic ceiling, the heart of the former Moorish palace, and in fact one of the oldest surviving parts of the Alhambra.

Opposite: The Parador of San Francisco, within the Alhambra precinct and formerly the Monastery of San Francisco. Below: The Catholic Monarchs, Ferdinand and Isabel. (From a painting in the convent at Madrigal de las Altas Torres, where Isabel was born.)

One of the charms of staying at the Parador is that it lies within the actual precinct and its grounds merge with those of the Alhambra, which in turn adjoin the cool gardens of the Generalife, with their cypresses, roses, arching fountains and tumbling waters, and the delicate *miradores*, high above the city and its distant green *vega*. In the words of the Emperor Charles V, 'Ill-fated is the man who lost all this!'

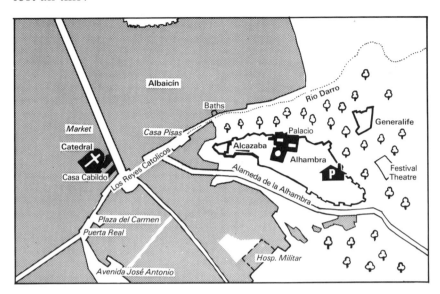

Granada is, of course, in Andalusia; and the Parador serves a selection of regional dishes. After a morning spent in clambering around the Alhambra, a refreshing start is the *Gazpacho al ajo blanco*, a cold soup containing ground almonds, garlic and a little vinegar and olive oil. The Parador is near the sea, the lifeline of its Moorish occupants—and the *Sopa de pescado malagueña* (fish soup, Málaga style) or *Zarzuela de pescado motrileña* (for Zarzuela, see pages 61 and 34; Motril is the nearest port) are both appetizing and well-made. The *vega*, where Ferdinand established his camp, has always been known for its fruit and vegetables; and this is reflected in the *Macedonia de legumbres de la vega* (mixed vegetables), *Huevos al plato granadina* (eggs with broad beans and ham), and the fresh fruit salad. The *filete de ternera andaluza* is veal cooked in regional style; and from the Albaicín, the gipsy quarter across the ravine from the Alhambra, come the *Hojaldres*, one of those pastries at which the Moors excelled.

There are other modern Paradores in Andalusia, which offer a further choice of regional cooking. At Arcos de la Frontera near Jerez, a town of narrow alleys and white houses long in the hands of the Moors, try the famous *Sopa gaditana* (Cadiz style soup) made with a basis of chicken broth and containing hard-boiled egg, ham, garlic and sherry. Other specialities here are the *Riñones al Jerez* (kidneys sautéed in sherry) and the *Fritura de pescado a la gaditana* (mixed fried fish). On gastronomic maps Andalusia is often labelled 'The Zone of Frying'; and this is one of the best dishes of its long coastline. In terms of fish, it corresponds to a mixed grill, and apart from a variety of crisp-fried

130

whitefish, usually contains sardines, fresh anchovies and inkfish.

Nearer to Granada, and a convenient halting place on the way to Seville or Cordoba, the small Albergue at Antequera boasts an astonishingly inventive menu. The *Remojón antequerano* is a salad consisting of sliced orange, olives and onion, garnished with chopped hard-boiled egg and flaked *bacalao*. Its *Budins de pescado* are made of different types of whitefish, flaked and mixed with onion and grated carrot, beaten up with eggs, then cooked and served with a lobster sauce. In season, the baby rabbits are entirely delicious.

The typical wine of Andalusia is, of course, sherry—and to a lesser degree Montilla, made near Córdoba by the same *solera* system, but not fortified. A cool dry Montilla, although stronger than a normal table wine, can be and frequently is, drunk throughout a meal.

The Parador at Arcos de la Frontera and M.I.T.'s Hotel Atlántico in Cadiz are both conveniently placed for a visit to the sherry bodegas at Jerez de la Frontera, a trip very well worth making, if only to taste the astonishing fragrance of sherry when drunk on the spot. Visitors are welcome at almost all the bodegas during working hours in the morning; and the tour ends with a generous tasting.

The region does not produce any ordinary table wines of note; but the Parador carafes, with the all-pervading 'nose' of sherry, are often pleasant—and less heady.

Overleaf left: View from the Parador at Arcos de la Frontera. Overleaf right: Views of the Parador of San Francisco. Right: The last page of the treaty of 1491 agreeing the surrender of Granada, with the signatures of the Catholic Monarchs and their secretary, Fernando de Zafra.

GAZPACHO ANDALUZ

A favourite cold soup from Andalusia
2 red peppers
1 clove of garlic
Salt
½lb (250gm) tomatoes
5oz (140gm) toasted breadcrumbs
2 tablespoons refined olive oil
4 tablespoons vinegar

Remove the seeds and capsules from the peppers. Squeeze in the garlic, add a little salt and grind into a paste. Add the chopped tomatoes and breadcrumbs, moistened in water, and grind until smooth. Drip in the olive oil drop by drop, stirring continuously. Now stir a little water into the paste and rub it through a sieve.

If you have a blender you can save yourself a great deal of elbow grease by using it for all these operations.

Finally, add 2½ pints (1½ litres) of cold water, stir in the vinegar and serve well-chilled with cubes of bread on the side.

MERLUZA AL ESTILO DE LA ALHAMBRA
HAKE ALHAMBRA STYLE

Serves 4
2 cloves garlic, chopped
Salt
2 dessertspoons olive oil
3oz (90gm) butter
2½oz (75gm) breadcrumbs
A little chopped parsley
Juice of 1 lemon
2lb (1kg) hake, in fillets

Marinate the fish in a glass dish with the garlic, salt and olive oil, leaving it in a cool place for 2 hours. Now dot an oven dish with the butter, lay the fillets on the bottom and sprinkle them with breadcrumbs, parsley and lemon juice. Leave for another hour, then cook in a preheated oven at 350°F (Mark 4) for 30 minutes.

132

Left: The Alhambra: The Torre de Siete Suelos and a view of the walls (from a painting by Richard Ford).

REMOJON
A salad from Antequera
2oz (60gm) *bacalao* (salted and dried cod)
8 green olives, stoned
2 hard-boiled eggs, sliced
1 orange, peeled and thinly sliced
1 small onion, cut into circles
Salt and pepper
Soak the *bacalao* overnight, remove the bones and flake. Mix all the ingredients in a bowl and then toss with a vinaigrette sauce, to which has been added a little sweet paprika.

Salsa vinagreta
1 small clove garlic, peeled
2 tablespoons refined vinegar
$\frac{1}{2}$ teaspoon salt
$\frac{1}{2}$ teaspoon made mustard
$\frac{1}{4}$ teaspoon white pepper
1 teaspoon sweet paprika
4 tablespoons refined olive oil
Squeeze the garlic into the vinegar, mix in the salt, mustard and pepper, then add the oil and stir vigorously until it forms an emulsion.

BUDIN DE PESCADO
FISH PUDDING
Serves 6
2lb (1kg) hake
1 onion
Parsley
Salt and pepper
2 tablespoons olive oil
12oz (340gm) tomatoes, blanched, peeled and cut up
134

1 teaspoon castor sugar
2oz (60gm) breadcrumbs, soaked in milk
4 eggs
Butter

Put the hake into a *cazuela* or pan with the white wine, half the onion, the parsley and a little salt and pepper. Simmer gently until tender for about 20 minutes, then take out the fish, remove the skin and bones and reserve on a plate.

Heat the olive oil in a pan and fry the rest of the onion, finely chopped, until it begins to colour; then add the tomatoes and sugar, cover with a lid and cook slowly for about $\frac{1}{2}$ hour. Rub this tomato sauce through a sieve and mix it with the fish, the moist breadcrumbs, the yolks of the eggs and a little salt and pepper. Stir well with a wooden spoon so as to make a purée. Whisk the whites of the eggs until stiff and fold into the mixture.

Now lightly grease an oven mould with butter, pour the mixture into it and place in a Bain Marie or saucepan of boiling water. Cook in a very moderate oven for about 1 hour. To test when the pudding is ready, push a knitting needle into it. If the mixture sticks to it, further cooking is necessary, but if it comes out clean, the pudding is done. At this point, remove the mould and invert the pudding on to a serving dish.

Below: Views of the Parador of San Francisco.

Sauce
2oz (60gm) prawns, peeled and cooked
2oz (60gm) butter
1oz (30gm) flour
½ pint (3dl) milk
Salt and pepper
Melt the butter in a saucepan, stir in the flour and add the milk, so as
to make a white sauce. Season with salt and pepper. Finally, add the
prawns and pour over the pudding.

RIÑONES AL JEREZ
KIDNEYS IN SHERRY
Serves 4
2lb (1kg) lambs' kidneys, free of fat
Vinegar
Butter
½ pint (3dl) *salsa española* (see below)

Left: Moorish remains inside the Parador of San Francisco, one of the earliest parts of the Alhambra. Opposite: One of the decorative menu covers, common to the different Paradores. Overleaf: A menu from the Parador of the Condes de Villalba.

136

MINISTERIO DE INFORMACION Y TURISMO

SERVICIO A LA CARTA

SERVICE A LA CARTE

Consomés, Entremeses	PRECIO
1 Caldo o crema a la gallega (*)	
2 Entremeses Parador	
3 Consomé tres filetes	
4 Sopa de rabo de buey	

Huevos

5 Huevos con zorza (*)	
6 Tortilla a la gallega (*)	
7 Huevos fritos con bacon	

Legumbres y Verduras

8 Espárragos dos salsas (220 grs.)	
9 Fabada asturiana (conserva)	
10 Zanahorias a la crema	
11 Judías verdes salteadas con jamón	

Pastas y Arroz

12 Empanada gallega (Pescado o Raxo) (*)	
13 Paella valenciana (30 minutos)	
14 Canelones Rossini	
15 Tallarines con tomate	

Pescados

16 Merluza a la gallega (*)	
17 Caldeirada gallega (*)	
18 Besugo al horno (*)	
19 Conchas de Peregrino (Vieiras) (*)	
20 Calamares rellenos (*)	
21 Pulpo a feira (*)	
22 Gambas al ajillo	

Carne, Aves y Caza

23 Brocheta de ternera "Don Nuño" (300 grs.) (*)	
24 Lacon con grelos (*)	
25 Jamon asado al Jerez (*)	
26 Callos a la gallega (*)	
27 Chuleta de ternera (300 grs)	
28 Entrecote (250 grs)	
29 Escalope San Jacobo	
30 Bistec de ternera	
31 Chuleta de cerdo frita	
32 Conejo a la casera	
33 Pepitoria de ave	

Postres

34 Queso del país (*)	
35 Filloas (*)	
36 Tarta (de Mondoñedo (*) o helada)	
37 Tocinillo de cielo	
38 Fruta del tiempo (3 piezas)	
39 Pudding al chocolate	
40 Helado variado	

Servicio e impuestos incluidos

Consommés, Hors-D'Oeuvre	PRIX
1 Potage ou crème à la Galicien (*)	
2 Hors-d'oeuvre	
3 Consommé "trois filets"	
4 Soupe à la queue de boeuf	

Oeufs

5 Oeufs frits au "zorza" (*)	
6 Omelette à la Galicienne (*)	
7 Oeufs frits au bacon	

Legumes

8 Asperges deux sauces (220 grs)	
9 Haricots blancs avec viande de porc	
10 Carottes à la crème	
11 Haricots verts sautés au jambon	

Pates et Riz

12 Pâte à la Galicienne (Poisson ou filet de porc) (*)	
13 Riz a la Valencienne (30 minutes)	
14 Cannellonis Rossini	
15 Pâtes à la tomate	

Poissons

16 Colin à la Galicienne (*)	
17 "Caldeirada" à la Galicienne (*)	
18 Dorade au four (*)	
19 "Vieiras" (Coquilles de Saint-Jacques) (*)	
20 Calamars farcis (*)	
21 Poulpe à la Feire (*)	
22 Crevettes à l'ail	

Viandes, Volailles et Gibier

23 Brochette de veau (300 grs) (*)	
24 "Lacón con grelos" (*)	
25 Jambon rôti ua sauce de vin de Xérés (*)	
26 Tripes à la Galicienne (*)	
27 Côtelette de veau (300 grs.)	
28 Entrecôte (250 grs.)	
29 Escalope de veau "San Jacobo"	
30 Bifteck de veau	
31 Côtelette de porc	
32 Lapin à là maison	
33 Ragoût de poulet	

Desserts

34 Fromage du pays (*)	
35 Crêpes à la Galicienne (*)	
36 Tarte (de Mondoñedo (*) ou glacé)	
37 Crème de jaune d'oeuf	
38 Fruits de la saison (3 fruits)	
39 Pudding au chocolat	
40 Glaces variées	

Service et taxes compris

Right: The chapel within the Parador of San Francisco, where the Reyes Católicos were first buried.

2 glasses dry sherry
1 clove garlic, crushed
Wash the kidneys and soak for 1 hour in cold water and vinegar. Drain and rinse, remove the skin and membranes and cut into thin slices with scissors. Fry for 5 minutes in salted butter, turning from time to time. Have ready a *cazuela* or casserole containing the *salsa española*. Add the kidneys, sherry and garlic and stew very slowly for 20 minutes.

Salsa española
This is the basic Spanish sauce, of wide application.
Olive oil
2 large onions, chopped
2 fresh or canned red peppers, chopped
1lb ($\frac{1}{2}$kg) tomatoes, or a 14oz (400gm) can
1 clove garlic, crushed
Salt and pepper
1 glass dry sherry
Pour some olive oil into a large frying pan. Add the onions and fry gently in the hot oil. When the onion is half-cooked, add the peppers, removing the capsule and seeds if the peppers are fresh, and continue the slow frying for about 20 minutes until they are tender. Then tilt the pan, retaining the vegetables with a spoon, and drain off the excess oil, which may be kept for further use. Once again, spread the onions and peppers over the surface of the pan and add the tomatoes. Fry slowly until all the ingredients form a pulp, finally adding the garlic and salt and pepper to taste. Put the mixture into a blender or pass it through a sieve and stir the sherry into it.

Ferdinand granted the Moors of Granada generous terms and in particular undertook to respect their religious beliefs. For five years the conditions of the capitulation were strictly honoured; but with the arrival of Queen Isabel's confessor, Archbishop Ximénez de Cisneros, a policy of forced baptism was instituted. In the climate of opinion in Christian Spain, it was perhaps inevitable. As early as 1391 the Jewish quarters of the large cities had been sacked; and there was a repetition of the pogroms in 1473. Both Jews and Muslims who were converted to Christianity remained suspect; and an Inquisition, set up in Castile to investigate the bona fides *of the 'New Christians', celebrated its first* auto de la fe *in Seville on 6 February 1481, with the burning of six of the most influential converts. No one who could not prove* limpieza de sangre *(or purity of blood) was admitted to office in the Church or to positions of public authority. The net result was to drive out many of the country's most skilled and hard-working inhabitants, who were essential for Spain's future prosperity. In a country where races were inextricably mixed it was the high-born who escaped the net. Ironically enough, it is said that even Ferdinand the Catholic had Jewish blood; and this was certainly true of Tomás de Torquemada, the first and most notorious Inquisitor General.*

Hostería del Pintor Zuloaga: Pedraza de la Sierra

It is in a house dating from this period, the so-called Casa de la Inquisición, that M.I.T. has installed the Hostería del Pintor Zuloaga at Pedraza de la Sierra. It is typical of the many beautiful fifteenth-century seignorial houses in this village north of Segovia. Today, the old conflicts are forgotten and the place has become something of a quiet colony of artists and writers, as well as a centre for hunting, fishing and winter sports in the surrounding mountains. The Hostería (which serves meals, but has no rooms) takes its name from Ignacio Zuloaga, a Spanish painter active during the first decades of this century, and one time owner of the fifteenth-century Castle of the Constables of Velasco in La Pedraza.

The Hostería del Pintor Zuloaga, traditionally known as the *Casa de la Inquisición*, or Inquisitor's House.

The restaurant is a favourite with weekend visitors from Madrid and is well known for its cooking in the Segovian style. One of its specialities is the *Caldereta* or lamb stew; but perhaps the most famous dish from this region is *Cochinillo asado* (roast sucking pig), a piglet which has been fed on nothing but milk and is opened, stuffed, and roasted in a baker's oven. If you do not wish to venture as far from Madrid as La Pedraza, this dish can be eaten to perfection at the Mesón de Candido, tucked beneath the great Roman aqueduct in Segovia itself. It is no idle boast that the meat is so tender that it can be cut with the rim of a plate.

Segovia is not a wine-growing province, so it is a question of drinking either a bottled Rioja or carafe wine, which one may safely assume to have come from Valdepeñas—and none the worse for it!

141

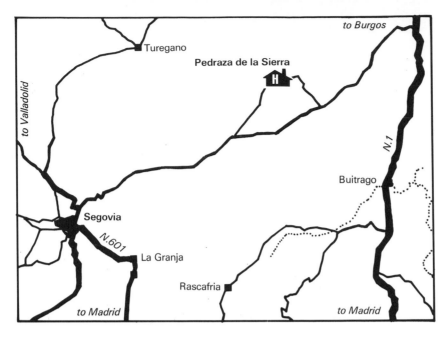

COCIDO CASTELLANO

This stew is one of the classical dishes of Spain and is made in different
variations in many parts of the country. It is served on separate plates
as soup, vegetables and meat, and is a meal in itself.

Serves 6 to 8

10oz (300gm) dried chick peas
Salt
Bicarbonate of soda
1lb (½kg) shin of beef
2 marrow bones
5oz (150gm) end of a ham bone
5oz (150gm) fresh belly of pork
1 turnip
3 leeks
2 carrots
2lb (1kg) cabbage
2 tablespoons olive oil
1 clove garlic, chopped
2oz (60gm) *estrellita*, a pasta made especially for soups. (Use whatever
   pasta is locally available.)
½lb (¼kg) potatoes, peeled
5oz (150gm) *chorizo*

Soak the chick peas overnight in tepid water containing a little salt and
a pinch of bicarbonate of soda. Next day, tie them up in muslin, so
that they do not disintegrate when cooked with the other ingredients.

   Put the meat and bones into a heavy stewpan, cover with water and
bring briskly to the boil. Immerse the chick peas in their muslin bag,
add a little salt, remove the froth with a spoon, then lower the heat,
cover and cook slowly for 1 hour. Now add the belly of pork, the turnip,
leeks and carrots and simmer for a further 2 hours, making good the
water lost by evaporation. Add the *chorizo* and the whole peeled

142

potatoes to the contents of the stewpot for the last $\frac{1}{2}$ hour of cooking.

Meanwhile, using a separate saucepan, boil the cabbage in lightly salted water for 15 minutes and drain it.

Heat a little olive oil in another saucepan, briefly fry the chopped garlic and add the cabbage, stirring it well and covering with a lid until heated through.

Half an hour before serving the meal, remove enough stock from the stewpan to make the soup and boil it with the pasta. 10 minutes will be enough if the pasta is of small size.

The *cocido* is served as follows:

1. Serve the soup
2. Withdraw the chick peas in their muslin bag from the stewpot and empty them on to a serving dish, arranging the potatoes on one side and the cabbage on the other.
3. On a separate dish, serve the meat, belly of pork, *chorizo*, ham and forcemeat (see below).

Relleno or forcemeat for cocidos
3 eggs
3oz (90gm) fresh breadcrumbs
1 large tablespoon parsley
1 clove of garlic, crushed
Salt and pepper
Olive oil for frying
Break the eggs into a bowl, add the fresh breadcrumbs, parsley and crushed garlic together with a little salt and pepper and mix well with a wooden spoon. Now shape the stiff mixture into balls, flatten with your hands and fry in hot olive oil until golden.

These forcemeat cakes are put into the stewpan and cooked with the *cocido* for the last 10 minutes before serving.

Below: The Cathedral at Segovia, near Pedraza de la Sierra.

Although Cardinal Ximénez de Cisneros was the scourge of the Moriscos in Granada, he was a great deal less bigoted in his views than Tomás de Torquemada. Emerging from monastic seclusion to become the most powerful prelate in Spain, he attacked the abuses of the ecclesiastical Establishment and enforced reform of the monasteries. After the death of Isabel the Catholic in 1504, he was appointed regent to the mad Queen Juana and a few years later founded the University of Alcalá de Henares, for long one of the most liberal in the country. At its height it numbered 12,000 students, rivalling Salamanca; and one of its great achievements was the printing of the first polyglot Bible during 1514 to 1520—the famous Complutense, *so-called from the Roman name for Alcalá,* Complutum. *Among the university's illustrious alumni were the dramatists Lope de Vega and Tirso de Molina; the satirist Quevedo; the founder of the Society of Jesus, Ignacio de Loyola; the philosopher, Spínola; and the liberal statesman, Jovellanos. Alcalá was also the birthplace of the great Cervantes. The Universidad Complutense was closed early in the nineteenth century, but has again opened its doors as a centre for studies in public administration.*

Hostería del Estudiante: Alcalá de Henares

The Hostería del Estudiante, half-an-hour's drive north from Madrid, forms part of the ancient Colegio Trilingüe, so-called because it was devoted to the study of Latin, Greek and Hebrew. It was opened in 1548 as part of Ximénez's original foundation of 1508, the College of San Ildefonso, whose magnificent Baroque facade, reconstructed in 1543, can be seen nearby. In 1588 the Colegio Trilingüe was rehoused in the present building, which dates from 1557. Reminiscent of the quiet, cloistered quadrangles of Salamanca, it is a low structure of mellow stone, supported by thirty-six arches and looking into a courtyard, at the centre of which is the original well with deeply indented decoration in the form of scallop shells. On summer nights this courtyard forms an atmospheric setting for open-air banquets and presentations of the classical Spanish theatre.

Opposite the part of the building used for the Hostería is the *Paraninfo* or college hall, a large room, part Mudéjar, part Renaissance, with a richly carved and painted ceiling and ornate stucco work, dating from the time of Ximénez. This is still used for degree ceremonies, and it is easy to envisage the former graduands of the Universidad Complutense in their blue robes and scarlet hoods.

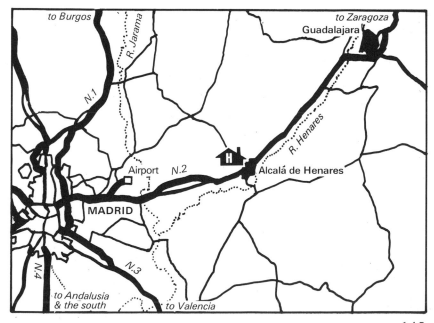

By the eighteenth century the number of students at the Colegio Trilingüe had so declined that the building was sold and converted into quarters for old people. In 1929 the Patronato Nacional de Turismo restored the patio and opened the Hostería. Unfortunately, the building like the rest of Alcalá, suffered serious damage during the Civil War, but was once again faithfully and lovingly restored and has been in use as an Hostería since the mid-forties.

The restaurant is installed in a large room on the ground floor. As to its white-washed walls, great chimney piece, saddle bags, mule chairs and wine-skins, it is difficult to improve on the inimitable French of the *Guide Bleu*: '*Il offre une charmante reconstitution d'auberge castillane du XVe s.*'

Below: The courtyard of the Hostería del Estudiante, once part of the Colegio Trilingüe of the University of Alcalá de Henares.

Above: Cardinal Ximénez de Cisneros, who founded the University of Alcalá de Henares in 1508 (from *Recuerdos de un Viage por España*, 1849).

Like the Hostería at Pedraza de la Sierra, the restaurant is a favourite rendezvous for *Madrileños* at weekends, when it is always crowded. All the typical Castilian cuisine may be sampled here and also such universal Spanish favourites as *Bacalao al pil-pil* (dried, salted cod with chillis), *Merluza a la vasca* (Basque style hake with asparagus) and *Truchas a la Navarra* (trout with ham—see page 45). Among its regional dishes, the menu singles out *Huevos con migas y tropezones* (eggs with fried breadcrumbs); *Cordero asado* (roast lamb); *Chuletitas de cordero* (small lamb chops); *Sopas de ajo* (garlic soups); and *Callos* (tripe). *Callos a la madrileña* are prepared in very different style from the tripe in Galicia or Portugal (see page 119). It is cut into thin strips and served in the most piquant of sauces, containing onion. tomato, ham, *chorizo* and chilli powder. After this fiery, but highly individual concoction, the menu is perhaps wise in recommending *Natillas con pestiños* (custard with fritters) or *Arroz con leche* (milky rice pudding). There are no local wines; and, as in Madrid, the carafe wine is from the extensive vineyards of La Mancha to the south. The restaurant possesses a large cellar and can also provide vintage wines from many of the better-known regions, including some fine old Riojas and an array of brandies, French and Spanish. Among the Spanish, 'Lepanto' is to be highly recommended; a less expensive but palatable '*coñac*' is that from the excellent Catalan firm of Torres.

CALLOS A LA MADRILEÑA
TRIPE MADRID STYLE
Serves 4
2lbs (1kg) cleaned boiled tripe
2 pig's trotters
1 red pepper
Olive oil
1 onion, chopped
1 tomato, peeled and sliced
8oz (225gm) cooked ham, chopped
1 clove of garlic, chopped
½ teaspoon chilli powder
2 or 3 chunks *chorizo*
Salt
Buy boiled and cleaned tripe and cut it into thin strips. Simmer for 1 hour 30 minutes in salted water, together with the pig's trotters, previously blanched in boiling water and well scraped.

Take out the trotters with a draining spoon, put them on a plate and separate the tender meat from the bones. Return this meat to the saucepan with the tripe.

Remove the seeds from the red pepper, cut it into strips and fry in olive oil with the onion and tomato until soft. Add the ham, garlic, chilli powder, chunks of *chorizo* and salt. Stir well, then pour the sauce into the stewed tripe—by now the original amount of water will be much reduced—and simmer gently for another 10 to 15 minutes.

147

After the death of Isabel the Catholic in 1504, her husband Ferdinand acted as regent, since their daughter Joan (Juana la Loca) was feeble-minded and unfit to rule. Her son by Philip of Austria, Charles I, became the first of Spain's Hapsburg rulers when Ferdinand died in 1516. Within three years, on the death of his paternal grandfather, Maximilian I, he was also elected Holy Roman Emperor as Charles V, and it is under this name that he is best known.

From the early 1520s Charles was occupied with grandiose campaigns abroad—against Francis I in France and Italy; in Germany, where he was the champion of Catholicism against the Lutherans; and in the Mediterranean, against the Barbary Corsairs and the Turks. But on his arrival in Spain, he had first to put his own house in order. There was considerable opposition on the part of the Comunidades, *the great incorporated municipalities of Castile, to the Burgundians and Flemings to whom Charles gave positions of authority. The bourgeoisie and urban gentry rose against the King and the nobility in a revolt which was put down only after a pitched battle at Villalar in 1521.*

Virrey de Toledo: Oropesa

The leader of the so-called *Comuneros*, Juan Padilla, was assisted by the Counts of Oropesa; and their castle, now the Parador of the Virrey of Toledo, became a main base for the rebellion. Charles had Padilla and other ring-leaders of the revolt executed and threatened the Count of Oropesa, don García Alvarez de Toledo, with the destruction of his fortress. It nevertheless survived intact, as it had done earlier, when the first Count took sides against Isabel, supporting the claim of Juana la Beltrejana to the throne of Castile and thereafter incurring the wrath of the Catholic Monarchs.

Oropesa was the scene of fierce fighting between the Christians and the Moors; and there is a legend that the place took its name from *a peso de oro* ('its weight in gold'), referring to the ransom of

The keep and walls of the Castle of Oropesa.

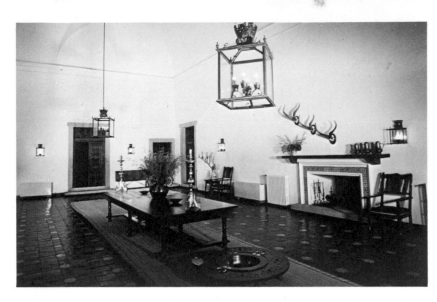

Left: A salon in the Parador of
the Virrey de Toledo.

a Christian princess. In 1366 Pedro the Cruel ceded the castle to
the Duke of Frías, don García Alvarez de Toledo, who proceeded
to make good the damage inflicted during the struggles of the
Reconquest.

The square lay-out with its massive battlemented walls and
round corner towers dates from this period; the further rectangular
structure and spacious *plaza de armas* or parade ground, now used
for open-air festivals, were added in 1402. The castle, crowning a
small hill on the edge of the Sierra de Gredos, is a landmark for

Below: From the balcony of the
Parador.

miles around and remained in its pristine state of repair until severely damaged during the Peninsular War.

The Parador is installed in the palace of the Counts of Oropesa and Dukes of Frías, connecting with the castle proper, and is named after don Francisco de Toledo (1512–82), who was for twelve years Viceroy of Peru. A tablet commemorating his achievements in the New World stands above the entrance stairway.

Writing in 1866, Richard Ford records that, 'The Duke of Frias, when a few years ago on a fortnight's visit to an English lady, never once troubled his basins and jugs; he simply rubbed his face occasionally with the white of an egg . . .' The present arrangement of the Parador, with its spacious marble-floored private bathrooms, air-conditioned bedrooms, magnificent series of reception rooms, and a balcony running the length of the building, cool even in the heat of a blazing Castilian summer, reflects a very different state of affairs. The view across the wide Tiétar Valley towards the distant rampart of the Sierra de Gredos must be among the most beautiful from any of the Paradores; and Oropesa, only an hour and a half from Madrid on its tranquil hilltop, is the ideal place for a quiet, unworldly weekend.

Right: Before the Emperor Charles V began his grandiose campaigns in Europe he had first to put in order his own house in Spain, and among his principal opponents were the Counts of Oropesa. Titian's portrait shows him at the Battle of Mühlberg, 1548.

151

As befits the torrid summers, the Parador serves a variety of cold soups: *Sopa de ajo blanco* (see page 124), *Gazpacho andaluz* (see page 132) and its own speciality, *Gazpacho de pastor*. The main dishes reflect the local abundance of game and fish and include trout from the River Tormes, either fried with ham (*Truchas del Tormes fritas*) or marinated (*Truchas escabechadas*), *Codornices del coto de doña Ana* (quail) and *Conejo de la Dehesa Nueva* (rabbit). Especially recommended is its roast lamb (*Cordero asado 'Tio Gildo'*). Among the sweets are the cream puffs charmingly named *Suspiros de monja* (Nun's sighs) and *Tocinillo de*

cielo, surprisingly translated as 'Salt Pork Sky'! In sober fact, this is a confection made from egg yolks and sugar flavoured with vanilla in the manner of creme caramel.

Oropesa is on the fringe of the great wine-growing region of La Mancha, known for bulk rather than quality; and on the high road to Madrid one passes near the dusty township of Méntrida, where the bodegas stand cheek by jowl, the source of the local *vino corriente* (*vin ordinaire*).

Below: The facade and entrance of the Parador of the Virrey de Toledo.

PISTO MANCHEGO

This somewhat resembles the French *ratatouille*. It may accompany roast meats or, with an egg broken into it, is a main course on its own.

Serves 4

Olive oil
1 large onion, sliced
1lb ($\frac{1}{2}$kg) green peppers
1lb ($\frac{1}{2}$kg) courgettes (baby marrows)
1 potato, peeled and sliced
1lb ($\frac{1}{2}$kg) tomatoes, blanched and peeled (or equivalent of canned tomatoes)
1 clove of garlic, crushed
Salt
1 egg per person (optional)

Put a little olive oil into a large *cazuela* or stewpan and fry the onion slowly for 3 to 4 minutes. Remove the seeds from the peppers, cut into small pieces and add. Next add the potato and cook for another 2 or 3 minutes before addition of the courgettes, washed and cut into small rounds.

Drain off all excess oil and stir in the tomatoes, which will provide sufficient liquid for further cooking. Season with garlic and a little salt. Simmer slowly for about 1 hour 30 minutes. Break in the eggs, if desired, a minute or two before serving.

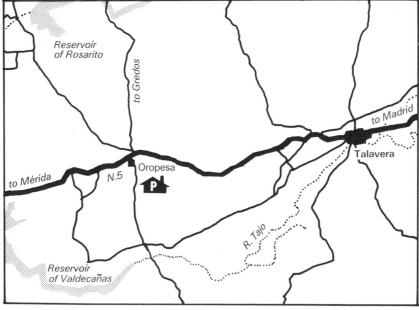

While the Emperor Charles V threw himself into the task of upholding Catholicism in Europe, the exploration and conquest of America proceeded apace. The completion of the Reconquest had left Spain with a reservoir of fighting men, who for reasons of pride and a disinclination to compete with the hard-working Moriscos, *or Christianized Moors, swelled the ranks of the* Conquistadores. *It has been said that the discovery of the Americas was absolutely necessary for Spain, to provide a new outlet for the energies of its Christian inhabitants. The largest exodus was from the Extremadura on the Portuguese border; even today its high sierras, with their roaming flocks of sheep, remain empty and sparsely inhabited. The conquerors of both Mexico and Peru, Cortés (1485–1547) and Pizarro (1478–1541) were from this region.*

In his youth Cortés was a protégé of the Duke of Feria, the lords of the Castle of Zafra, perhaps the most magnificent of the region and now named the Parador de Hernán Cortés in his honour. It was here that he lived before his high spirits and love of adventure led him westwards, first to Santo Domingo to join his relative, Ovando, governor of Hispaniola, and later to take part in the expedition to Cuba and become conqueror of Mexico.

Hernán Cortés: Zafra

The site is an historic one and was fortified first by the Celto-Iberians and then by the Romans. When the Moors occupied the area they built an alcázar or castle, which they named *Zafar* (from the Arabic *Safar*, meaning June) in celebration of a festival held at that time of year. The present building, begun by Lorenzo de Figueroa in 1437 and finished in 1443, incorporates three distinct styles: the original Moorish; Gothic—as modified by Mudéjar craftsmen of Moorish origin; and classical Renaissance. The main entrance, which, with its flanking towers looks like something from a book of fairy tales, is part of the original fabric; carved above it are the twin shields of Lorenzo Suárez de Figueroa and his wife, doña María Manuel. The great interior courtyard, flanked by

The entrance to the Parador, one of the most magnificent castles in the Extremadura.

157

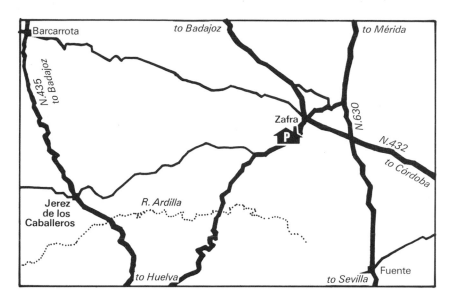

Doric columns in finely-worked white marble and supporting a glassed-in gallery, has been attributed to Juan de Herrera, the architect of the Escorial. The beautiful chapel with its octagonal cupola was added in the sixteenth century, as was the *sala dorada*, a noble chamber adorned with a richly carved and gilt ceiling, a notable example of the Moorish-inspired *artesonado* work.

Zafra (and also Mérida) is a convenient centre for visits to Medellín and Trujillo, the birthplaces of Cortés and Pizarro. The approach to Medellín over a fine seventeenth-century bridge across

Page 156: Typical dishes from the Hostería del Estudiante, whose restaurant is a favourite with the Madrileños.

Page 157
Above: The Renaissance patio of the Parador of Hernán Cortés, attributed to Juan de Herrera, architect of the Escorial. Below: The fine cloistered patio of the Parador of Carlos V.

Opposite: The air around Jarandilla is pungent with the fragrance of spice. The picture shows peppers drying in the sun before being milled into paprika powder. Right: The Church of San Bartolomeo at Jerez de los Caballeros, near Zafra, one of the last strongholds of the Knights Templars in Spain, with its extraordinary facade in crumbling stucco and blue tiles.

159

the Guadiana river, with the mediaeval castle rising above the little town, is magnificent; but the place itself is a little disappointing. A bronze in the dusty, sun-bleached square commemorates its illustrious son; and a stone slab marks the position of the house where he was born, long since pulled down.

The Plaza Mayor in Trujillo, flanked by arcades, enclosed by a rampart of fine baronial houses and dominated by the bulk of the castle, is one of the most evocative in Spain. At the centre is a modern statue of Pizarro, mounted on one of those horses which so astonished and terrified the Incas as to allow the conquest of their country by a handful of bold adventurers. Trujillo also possesses a number of fine churches; it is a place in which to linger, and the M.I.T. currently has plans for opening a Parador in a former convent.

Another worthwhile excursion from Zafra is westwards along the by-road into Portugal to the strange little town of Jerez de los

Above: A statue of Hernán Cortés at his birthplace, Medellín.

Left: The Church of San Bartolomeo at Jerez de los Caballeros.

160

Caballeros—the *Caballeros* in question being the Knights Templars. The ruins of their castle, from which they were driven in the early fourteenth century on the dissolution of the Order, still survive and are approached through a maze of steep and winding Moorish alleys impassable to motor traffic. Jerez de los Caballeros also has its connections with the *Conquistadores* and was the birthplace of Vasco Núñez de Balboa, the discoverer of the Pacific. Its most extraordinary monument is perhaps the Baroque tower of the Church of San Bartolomeo, intricately figured in crumbling stucco and vivid blue *azulecos*.

Right: The sixteenth-century chapel within the Parador of Hernán Cortés.

The Parador's menu is very similar to that of the *Via de la Plata* at Mérida—which is only some fifty kilometres to the north; but the cooking is less sophisticated. Among the regional specialities are *Gazpachos*, the cold garlic soup *Al Estilo de pastor extremeño*, the cured hams and *chorizos* mentioned in connection with Mérida (see page 44), *Migas* (savoury breadcrumbs, see page 46), *Caldereta* (ragout of lamb) and, in season, *Faisan relleno* (stuffed pheasant) and *Pastel de perdices* (partridge pie). The traditional cuisine was much influenced by the example of the monasterial tables—and not only in the sweetmeats for which they have always been famous. Regional sweets include a range of pancakes, cakes and fritters—*Tortas*, *Perrunillas*, *Frituras con miel* (also known as *Moñitas extremeñas* or 'little dolls'); but perhaps the best way to finish a meal is with the luscious watermelon from nearby Almendralejo.

Almendralejo is also the source of much of the carafe wine drunk in the region; with its serried bodegas it resembles nothing so much as another Valdepeñas. As in the Valdepeñas area of La Mancha, some of the large sherry concerns maintain distilleries for producing grape alcohol from the more ordinary wines for addition to sherry or for making brandy.

The *Tierra de Barros* around Almendralejo also produces some good wine; the whites from Pedro Ximénez, Palomino, Lairén, Moscatel and

161

Macabeo grapes, and above all from the Cayetana; and the reds from the Almendralejo, Garnacho and Morisca. Among the best red wines are those of Salvatierra de Barros—so-called because it once made domestic pottery, peddled throughout Spain, from the local *barro* or clay. These wines are aromatic, brilliant and intensely coloured; but to sample them, one must make a special journey to this remote village, some 20 kilometres off the road from Zafra to Jerez de los Caballeros.

FRITO TIPICO EXTREMEÑO
This is one of the fried dishes typical of the Extremadura.
Serves 4
Sweet paprika
2lb (1kg) leg of kid, boned and cut into large pieces
Olive oil
2 bay leaves
1 pint (6dl) dry white wine
4 cloves of garlic, crushed
Salt and pepper
Sprinkle the paprika powder on the pieces of meat. Heat some olive oil in a stewpan with the bay leaves, add the pieces of kid and fry until golden. Now add the wine, garlic and a little salt and pepper and cook slowly for about 1 hour until the meat is tender.

A village near Zafra, with typical white houses.

Thirty-five years of campaigning in Europe left Charles V with immense prestige. The Emperor personified the Castilian ideal of stemming the rising tide of Protestantism in Europe and threw the vast new resources from America into the struggle. With this in view he neglected the internal economy and strained his relations with the Cortes (parliament) by his incessant demands for money. He established a Spanish hegemony in Italy after the Battle of Pavia in 1525 and with his overwhelming victory at Mühlberg in 1547 cowed the German princes into submission and for a time imposed Catholicism on the country. Yet for all his dazzling victories in the field, he was unable to make a vassal of France, to halt the Ottoman Turks or to put an end to the depredations of the Corsairs in the Mediterranean, or in the last resort to catholicize Germany. Religion cannot be imposed by force of arms; and in the face of continuing revolt he was forced to concur with the decision of the Diet of Augsburg in 1555 that Catholics and Protestants should worship side by side in freedom.

In this same year, disappointed and weary of power, he abdicated, making over first the Low Countries and then Spain to his son Philip II. It was clear that the Germans would not tolerate a continuing union with Spain, so the title of Holy Roman Emperor went first to his brother Ferdinand and later to his bastard son Jeronimín, who as don Juan of Austria was later to win the decisive naval battle of Lepanto against the Turks.

Carlos V: Jarandilla de la Vera

In November 1555 Charles V arrived at the isolated castle of Jarandilla de la Vera, now the Parador of Carlos V, on the southern flank of the Sierra de Gredos, after taking ship from Brussels and then being carried across the mountains from Laredo in a litter. Here he took up residence until apartments were prepared for him in the neighbouring monastery of Yuste. It was a remote refuge but the Emperor certainly chose with an eye to natural beauty. The valley of the Tiétar and the mountain slopes above it are a symphony of colour with the contrasting greens of the pines and tobacco plantations, the startling yellow of the poplars in autumn and the full-blooded red of the wide fields of peppers.

The castle, which belonged to the Counts of Oropesa and the

Below: The entrance to the Parador of Carlos V. It was here that the Emperor Charles V arrived in 1555 after his voluntary abdication and stayed until apartments were made ready for him at the neighbouring Monastery of Yuste.

164

Marquesses of Jarandilla, is a rectangular building with solid battlemented towers at the corners, and dates from the late fourteenth century. It is built in local stone around a spacious courtyard, with a cloistered arcade and balcony at one end. Other features are the drawbridge, the beautiful *azulecos* (polychrome tiles) and a number of carved coats of arms, notably that of Alvarez of Toledo.

Some 18 kilometres to the west is the Monastery of Yuste, cool and secluded among its overgrown gardens and groves of towering eucalyptus. The approach to the royal suite, where Charles spent a brief year and a half before his death in 1558, is by a ramp constructed to afford the ailing Emperor the least inconvenience. The rooms, which are still hung in black from ceiling to floor in memory of his mother's death, contain many of his personal

Right: The gateway of the Parador of Carlos V.

belongings, including his invalid chair with adjustable foot-rest—to judge from its size, he must have been of diminutive stature. His deep religiosity imbues the apartments. Like his son Philip II. at the Escorial, he arranged for his bedrooms to communicate directly with the choir of the adjacent church, so that he could make his devotions without moving from his chamber. His original tomb (his remains were later removed to the Escorial) was constructed immediately below the high altar, so that the most humble of priests would in effect step on him when celebrating Mass.

Jarandilla, enfolded in tranquility and sheltered by the massif of the Sierra de Gredos from the brusque winds of Avila to the north, is the ideal place for complete quiet and relaxation. It is also a convenient base for expeditions to Guadalupe (see page 99) and Plasencia, with its noble cathedral.

Above: The Monastery of Yuste (from *Recuerdos de un Viage por España*, 1849).

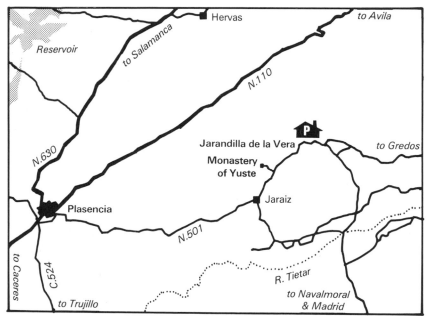

The Parador's menu is fairly extensive and apart from its own regional specialities includes such things as fillet steak and tournedos, *Parrillada de pescado* (mixed fried fish—see page 61), *Pollo a la chilindrón* (chicken in chilindrón sauce—see page 109), *Fabada asturiana* (see page 25) and *Callos a la madrileña* (Madrid style tripe, see page 147).

Among the regional specialities are *Bacalao al estilo de Yuste* (salted and dried cod beaten up with potato purée and butter), *Caldereta jarandillana* (a ragout of kid in white wine), *Sopa de mollejas* (a soup prepared from sweetbreads), *Pollo en pepitoria* (a well-known way of serving chicken with almond sauce) and *Arroz con leche a la canela* (caramelized rice spiced with cinnamon).

This is not a wine-growing area; the nearest source of *vino comun* (*vin ordinaire*) is Méntrida on the southern side of the Tiétar valley, which makes an acceptable carafe wine in bulk.

166

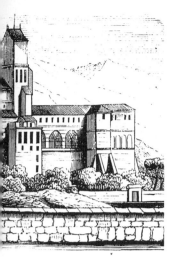

Right: A bedroom in the Parador of Carlos V.

BACALAO AL ESTILO DE YUSTE
BACALAO IN THE STYLE OF YUSTE
Serves 4
Bacalao is a form of dried and salted cod extremely popular in Spain—and even more so in Portugal, where it is said that there is a different method of preparing it for every day of the year. It is available abroad at specialized provision shops.

1lb 5oz (600gm) *bacalao*
14oz (400gm) potatoes, peeled and cut up
1oz (30gm) butter
Salt and pepper

Soak the *bacalao* overnight, changing the water from time to time. Next day remove the bones and skin and boil for 20 minutes with the potatoes. Now proceed as if making mashed potato, beating up the fish and potato with the butter (reserving a little to dot the top of the purée). Preheat the oven and cook at moderate heat (Mark 5, 375°F) for about 20 minutes until browned.

167

CALDERETA A LA JARANDILLANA
RAGOUT OF LAMB OR KID JARANDILLA STYLE
Serves 6
Olive oil
4 cloves of garlic
2lb (1kg) leg of lamb or kid
Sweet paprika powder
Salt and pepper
1 bay leaf
1 glass dry white wine
5oz (150gm) lambs' liver, cut up
Black pepper
1 red pepper, cut into strips

Heat some olive oil in a stewpan and cook two cloves of garlic until golden, then discard them. Cut the meat into small pieces, season with a little sweet paprika and salt, brown in the hot oil and add the bay leaf and wine. Cook for a few minutes, add sufficient water to make a thick sauce and continue simmering for ½ hour. Meanwhile fry the lambs' liver with the other two cloves of garlic, sprinkle on a little black pepper and add to the stewpan together with the strips of red pepper. Check the seasoning and cook for another ½ hour or until the meat is tender.

ARROZ CON LECHE A LA CANELA
CARAMELIZED RICE WITH CINNAMON
Serves 6
9oz (250gm) rice
1½ pints (1 litre) milk
7oz (200gm) castor sugar
1 vanilla pod
Lemon peel

Boil the rice for 5 minutes, drain and wash. Return to the saucepan with the milk, vanilla pod and lemon peel. Simmer for 10 minutes, then add 5oz (150gm) of the sugar and continue simmering for another 10 minutes. Turn out on to a dish and allow the rice to cool. Sprinkle with the remaining sugar and caramelize the top with a pallet knife heated in a gas ring. Sprinkle with cinnamon before serving.

'Charles V arrives at Yuste.' The litter in which he was carried from Laredo on the north coast is still preserved in Charles's apartments at the Monastery of Yuste (from a nineteenth-century painting by Alarcón).

Seen from a distance, Avila, behind its encircling wall, looks more like the dream of a mediaeval city than actual stone and mortar. Yet for all its mediaeval appearance, Avila will always remain the city of Santa Teresa. This remarkable woman, who inspired the leaders of the Counter-Reformation in Europe and whose work was largely responsible for preventing the spread of Protestantism to Spain, was born in 1515. She entered a Carmelite convent in 1533, but grew increasingly dissatisfied with the lax discipline of the religious orders and in 1562, in the face of stiff opposition, but with permission from the Pope, established a tiny convent in Avila, where the sisters, at first only four in number, lived according to the primitive rule. The number grew to thirteen and Santa Teresa took up her abode with them. Her energy and administrative ability later enabled her to found another fifteen houses and, with the help of St. John of the Cross, seventeen more, dedicated to the reform of the Carmelite friars. Together with her practical gifts and commonsense went the mystical graces that emerge in books like The Way of Perfection *and* The Castle of the Soul— *among the classics of Spanish literature.*

Raimundo de Borgoña: Ävila

The Parador of Raimundo de Borgoña is not associated with Santa Teresa, but with the era of Raymond of Burgundy, who first came to Spain in 1087 in a crusade against the Moors, later marrying a daughter of Alfonso VI and recapturing Avila from the Muslims. Count Raymond repopulated the city with his followers from Burgundy, León, Asturias and Galicia (there was a close connection with Cluniac confrères in Santiago de Compostela), so that it became known as *La Ciudad de los Caballeros*. The encircling walls, some 2,400 metres in extent and reinforced by 88 semi-circular towers, were built between 1090 and 1099 under the direction of a Master of Geometry, Casandro, and a French architect, Florin de Pituenga, probably with the enforced labour of Moorish captives. They incorporate not only the immensely solid apse of the cathedral (it is the highest bishopric in Europe) but also many of the baronial houses of Raymond's aristocratic following—and one such is the Parador itself, the former Palace of the Benavides, also known as the Palacio de Piedras Albas (Palace of White Stones).

The building underwent major reconstruction during the early years of this century, but certain features of the original structure remain, including the main stairway.

There is a great deal to see in Avila, beginning with the fortified cathedral, part Roman, part Gothic, with its massive granite exterior and an interior in which white stonework and red jasper are strangely contrasted. It is a city full of churches, both inside and outside the walls, many of them, of course, related to Santa Teresa.

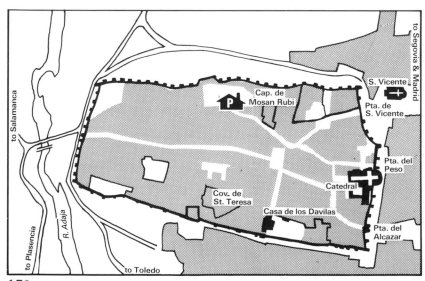

They include the Convent of Santa Teresa, the centre of her cult, which was built in 1636 on the site of the house where she was born and conserves the little garden where she played with her brothers and sisters; the Convent of Nuestra Señora de Gracia, where she was educated; the Convent of La Encarnación, where she lived for twenty years and which preserves some of her manuscripts; and the Convent of San José, her first foundation.

Avila (and also the Parador of Gredos, see page 213) are convenient centres for exploring the Sierra de Gredos, the rolling mountain region to the west of Madrid. Tucked away in the sheltered and luxuriant valleys are a number of charming villages and townships; among them are Piedrahíta, with its Gothic church and ruins of the palace belonging to the Dukes of Alba; Arenas de San Pedro and the nearby Castle of Mombeltrán, once the seat of the Dukes of Albuquerque; and El Barco de Avila, which also possesses a splendid mediaeval fortress.

Above: Santa Teresa of Avila (painting by Fray Juan de la Miseria from the Convent of Santa Teresa in Seville). Right: The evening *paseo* (promenade) outside the walls of Avila.

The cooking at the Parador is typical of Old Castile; and the menu lists such things as trout from the Tormes and Adajo rivers and traditional fare like *Cordero asado* (roast lamb), *Cocido* (a meat stew with chick peas) and *Cochinillo asado* (sucking pig roasted in a baker's oven). The veal (*ternera*), white and tender, is particularly good. The most famous local sweetmeat is the *Yemas de Santa Teresa*, made from egg yolks and sugar and typical of the confections made by the nuns in their convents. A more modern innovation is the *Tortilla Alaska*, ice cream thickly coated with beaten egg-white, which is then lightly browned in the oven or with a poker. But be warned! The menu specifies

171

that the portion is *para dos* (for two). When it arrives on its great salver, momentarily causing an astonished hush in the dining room, it is at once obvious that it would comfortably feed eight.

The carafe wine, from Cebreros in the Sierra de Gredos, is of great potency and can contain as much as 16 per cent alcohol.

COCHINILLO ASADO
ROAST SUCKING PIG
Serves 8 to 10
The sucking pig will already have been opened and cleaned by the butcher, and may be roasted either plain or stuffed.
Here is a Spanish recipe for the stuffing:
4oz (110gm) sausagemeat
8oz (225gm) cooked or smoked ham, chopped
The liver from the piglet, chopped
8oz (225gm) mushrooms, chopped
6 shallots, chopped
2 eggs, beaten
4oz (110gm) fresh breadcrumbs
1 tablespoon parsley, chopped
Salt and pepper
1 teaspoon mixed herbs
1 small glass aguardiente (or brandy)
Olive oil

Above left: The patio of the Parador of Raimundo de Borgoña.

Above right: The Parador was the former palace of the Benavides, and is built into the surrounding wall, like the Cathedral and many other baronial houses.

172

Thoroughly mix all the ingredients together (except the olive oil). Open the piglet, fill the cavity with the stuffing and sew it up with a strong needle and thread. Smear the outside with olive oil and coarse salt and stand on an oven rack in the roasting tin.

If unstuffed, the pig should simply be rubbed with oil and salt, opened and placed on the oven rack. It is also a good idea to put a bit of foil around the mouth and ears to prevent them blackening.

Make sure that the oven is really hot, and for an 8 to 10 pound ($3\frac{1}{2}$ to $4\frac{1}{2}$kg) sucking pig cook at moderate heat (375°F, Mark 5) for 2 hours 15 minutes to 2 hours 45 minutes, with an additional 15 minutes at 425°F, Mark 7, to crisp the outside. In Spain, where ovens are not always efficient, it is often the custom to take the pig to the local bakery for roasting.

Before carving, garnish with an apple in the mouth.

YEMAS DE SANTA TERESA

This sweetmeat, so typical of Avila and the surrounding district, may also be bought in the *confiterías*.

To make 12
3oz (90gm) castor sugar
1 stick of cinnamon
A little lemon peel
6 egg yolks
Icing sugar

Put the sugar, cinnamon and lemon peel into a small saucepan with 2fl oz (50ml) of water and heat until the sugar becomes thick and fibrous. Put the egg yolks into another saucepan and pour the mixture over them, stirring well with a wooden spoon. Cook gently until the paste begins to come away from the pan.

Turn out the contents on to a plate, and when cold cut into 12 portions with a knife. Tumble them in icing sugar and, as a refinement, serve them in paper cups.

Right: A passage in the Parador.

On the northern fringe of Andalusia are the twin towns of Ubeda and Baeza. Set among the olive groves near Linares where Manolete met his death in the bullring, these two towns reflect the splendour of the Spanish Renaissance. Ubeda has a special relationship with the House of Austria, since it was the birthplace of Francisco de los Cobos, principal secretary to the Emperor Charles V and adviser to Philip II in his youth. Until 1543, de los Cobos accompanied Charles on his expeditions the length and breadth of Europe; thereafter, he remained in Spain as financial adviser to the Prince, on whom the rule of the country increasingly devolved during his father's long absences abroad. While commending de los Cobos's acumen, Charles warned his son against following his example in marital affairs— de los Cobos was very much under the influence of an ambitious and domineering wife. It was perhaps her demands which earned him a reputation for venality in his later days. He retired to Ubeda, where he died shortly before the Emperor's abdication and return to Spain.

Right: Ubeda—the arches of the old town hall with the Romanesque Church of San Pablo beyond. Below: Girls at Ubeda dressed in traditional costume for the *fiestas*.

Above: View from the Parador of El Emperador looking towards Hendaye, with the Church of Santa María in the foreground, where in 1660 Maria Teresa of Austria was married to Louis XIV. Left: A hall in the Parador of El Emperador.

176

Condestable Davalos: Ubeda

The Parador of the Condestable Davalos, named after another illustrious contemporary, is installed in the former palace of Dean Ortega, a close associate of de los Cobos. De los Cobos's own Palacio de las Cadenas, now the townhall, lies a stone's throw away in the same noble stone-flagged square of Vázquez de Molina. The Constable in fact dwelt in yet another palace, the so-called Casa de las Torres. Behind the long sixteenth-century Baroque facade of the Parador lies a fine interior patio, green and cool in the heat of the Andalusian summer (nearby Ecija is reputedly the hottest place in Spain) with a balcony that preserves its old glass, giving access to the bedrooms.

Ubeda would be famous for the Plaza de Vázquez Molina alone, which has something of the theatrical quality of St. Mark's Square in Venice. At the same corner as the Parador is the Church of San Salvador, another foundation of Francisco de los Cobos. The

Below: The facade of the Parador of the Condestable Davalos.

richly sculptured Baroque portal of the church is one of the finest in Spain. Scattered about the town are numerous other baronial houses and churches worth the visit.

So completely was the place transformed during the sixteenth century that it is sometimes difficult to remember that the town was for long a stronghold of the Moors: it was on Ubeda that the shattered Almohad army fell back after its decisive defeat at Las Navas de Tolosa in 1212. One of the very few Moorish survivals is the charming little house with its 'horseshoe' arches, easily over-looked in a back alley, which now houses the Archaeological Museum. Its exhibits, including remarkable relics from the Palaeolithic era onwards and a wealth of Roman statuary, testify to an even more ancient past.

Baeza, only five miles away and not so long ago connected with Ubeda by a rural tramway running through the grey-green groves of olives, was also an important place under the Moors and knew dazzling prosperity during the sixteenth century. Its Baroque buildings, including the townhall, the Church of San Andrés, the Seminario de San Felipe Neri (formerly the Palace of the Bena-ventes), are hardly less splendid than those of Ubeda. The cathedral, built with a special dispensation from Pope Innocent IV to com-memorate Ferdinand the Saint's recapture of the town from the Moors, was reconstructed in the late sixteenth century, but now has sadly been abandoned.

178

Above: The Parador and the Church of San Salvador.

Opposite: The patio of the Parador.

Below: Francisco de los Cobos, principal secretary to the Em-peror Charles V and a native of Ubeda, responsible for some of its finest Baroque buildings (from an anonymous painting in the collection of the Duke of Alcalá, Madrid).

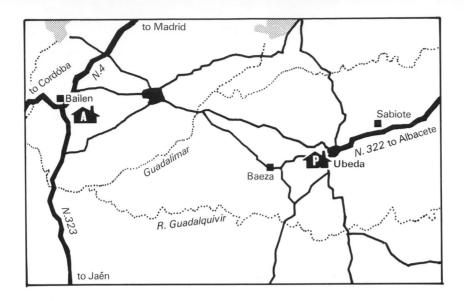

The regional cooking leans more towards that of Andalusia than that of La Mancha to the north. Variations of the cold *Sopa de ajo blanco*, sometimes containing hard-boiled egg, always figure on the Parador's menu. Since Ubeda is lost in a sea of olive trees, it is not surprising to find *Tajo redondo con aceitunas* (roast veal with olives) listed as a speciality. Then there are the spicy *Callos a la andaluza* (Andalusian style tripe) served with chick peas in a sauce made from tomatoes, onion, red peppers, *chorizo* and white wine; and *Pez espada a la parrilla* (grilled swordfish)—though this can sometimes be a little dry. Try the *Conejo de monte pastora* (rabbit) or *Codornices a la casera* (quail) during the season, when the olive groves ring to the Sunday fusilades of the *cazadores*. The Parador also serves a good *Tournedo Condestable*; and for the devotee of the quaint phrase, there are always 'Overcrusted macaronis' (*macaroni au gratin*)! The best of the sweets are *Leche frita* ('fried milk') and *Bizcocho borracho*, a tipsy cake made with brandy or sherry.

As a footnote to Parador food in general, it is virtually impossible for the ordinary foreign visitor to eat two large, and often highly spiced meals a day; perhaps the most sensible course is to experiment at lunch (which can be followed by a siesta) and order something light for supper. The consommés and egg dishes, including the varied types of *tortilla*, are always palatable.

There is no wine grown in Ubeda itself, but not so far to the north lie the vast vineyards of La Mancha, centring on Valdepeñas. For the wine-lover, it is worth the short diversion from the main road to Madrid to visit the bodegas of Valdepeñas and sample their wares. The Parador lists both red and white Manchego *a granel* (in bulk) and slightly more expensive Manchego *embotellado* (bottled). The best (though not the most expensive) red wine on the list is the Coronas Gran Reserva from Torres, a Catalonian wine which can often hold its own with a good Rioja or claret.

180

Right: A seignorial house in Ubeda with typical grilled windows.

LECHE FRITA
'FRIED MILK'
Serves 6
A favourite sweet
4 eggs
4oz (110gm) flour
4oz (110gm) castor sugar
½ pint (3dl) milk
1 stick cinnamon
A little butter
Olive oil
Beat two of the eggs and put into a saucepan with the flour, sugar, milk, cinnamon and a knob of butter. Stir well together and then cook over a low flame, continuing the stirring until the mixture is fairly thick. Turn out the contents of the pan on to a dish greased with butter, spreading them well out. Allow to cool. Cut into fingers, dredge in beaten egg and flour, then fry in hot oil until golden. Sprinkle with sugar and serve hot.

181

With the Emperor Charles V, the monarchy had taken upon its shoulders the burden of defending Catholicism. Spain was now the greatest military power in Europe; and the policy was continued with outward éclat during the reign of Charles's son, Philip II, El Prudente. *The Turks were defeated at Lepanto in 1571; the union with Portugal in 1581 led to the annexation of her vast colonial empire; revolt in the Low Countries was contained and France kept rigorously in check, so as to keep open communications with the Netherlands. In literature, too, it was the Golden Age of Cervantes and Lope de Vega.*

Only England challenged Spanish supremacy; and with the defeat of the Armada in 1588, the edifice cracked. Philip had neglected the economy, allowing the Genoese bankers to monopolize the profits from the exploitation of the American mines and foreign merchants to seize control of the colonial trade. His foreign adventures had brought the country to the verge of bankruptcy; and the long term result was to ensure the recovery of France as the major European power and to make inevitable the secession of Portugal.

His son, Philip III, was in no way the equal of his austere and single-minded father, and by acceding to the popular demand for the expulsion of the Christianized Moors and Moriscos in 1609, lost the country some 300,000 of its hardest-working citizens.

His successor, Philip IV, under the influence of the ambitious Count-Duke of Olivares, poured manpower and resources into a disastrous war with the Netherlands. A further attempt to impose a rigid centralism on the autonomous Kingdom of Catalonia gave a resurgent France the pretext for intervening in the Peninsula. The recurrent hostilities were only to end when the War of the Spanish Succession resulted in the enthronement of the first of the Spanish Bourbons in 1700.

El Emperador: Fuenterrabía

One of the most stirring episodes in the war with France, which broke out in 1635, was the heroic defence of Fuenterrabía and its fortress, now the Parador del Emperador, against an army under the Prince de Condé.

The little walled town of Fuenterrabía lies directly opposite Hendaye across the estuary of the River Bidassoa. In 1521, it had been captured by Francis I. However, at the time of the Prince de Condé's siege, the garrison repelled twenty attacks in sixty-four days. On 7 September, the eve of the Feast of the Nativity, Admiral Cabrera and the Marquess de los Vélez took the exhausted French troops by surprise and routed them. The victory, attributed to Nuestra Señora de Guadalupe is still celebrated at the sanctuary every year on the 8th of September.

The origins of this much-contested stronghold go back to the reign of King Sancho Abarca of Navarre (970–94) and it was extended by Sancho el Fuerte (1194–1234). During the centuries

Below: A lounge in the Parador.

Overleaf: The courtyard of the Parador of El Emperador. When it was reconstructed the trees were left growing from the wall.

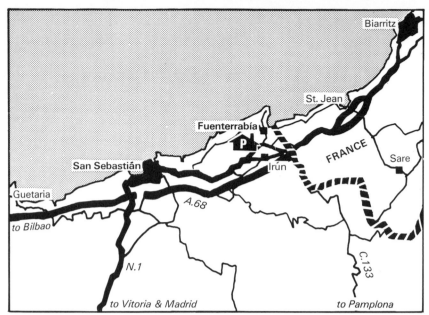

that followed it was strengthened by the Catholic Monarchs and rebuilt in its present form by the Emperor Charles V. It served both as a fortress and a royal palace and was frequented by Charles V, Philip III and Philip IV. In 1660 the Infanta María Teresa stayed in the palace before her wedding to Louis XIV in the adjoining church of Santa María de la Asunción; it was her grandson by this marriage who became the first of the Spanish Bourbons as Philip V.

The original walls and vaulting of the castle have survived, but the interior has been imaginatively reconstructed with great Gothic arches, winding stairs and galleries, an entrance hall, two large reception rooms and a bar occupying what was the fortress proper, and the bedrooms occupying the governor's palace. Much of the shaded central courtyard, with the cistern which supplied the garrison and townspeople with water during the many sieges, remains as it was, the trees growing out of the stonework bearing silent witness to past neglect. A flight of worn stone steps leads up to the battlements, from which there is a breathtaking view of Hendaye and the Bidassoa, dotted with pleasure-craft.

Fuenterrabía is a place of narrow, steeply-climbing streets flanked by baronial houses with overhanging balconies and great stone shields. Parts of the fifteenth-century walls survive; and the entrance is by the arched gateway of Santa María, surmounted by the town's coat of arms—two angels venerating the image of its patroness, Nuestra Señora de Guadalupe. Close to the frontier station of Irun, it is a most attractive place to spend the first or last night in Spain.

184

186

Naturally the different Paradores vary in the standard of their cuisine; of Fuenterrabía one can unreservedly say that it is of the best and that any dish on its menu is first-class. It is, of course, fortunate in being able to draw on the magnificent abundance of fish from the Bay of Biscay and the vegetables and dairy produce of the Basque area.

The *Sopa marinera* is an excellent *bisque*. If you are really hungry, try the *entremeses* (hors d'oeuvres) which include fresh anchovies, prawns fried with garlic and also in light batter, fried inkfish, savoury rissoles, egg croquettes, eggs with mayonnaise, small sausages, Russian salad, olives, cheese and radishes.

The fish ranges from fried fresh sardines stuffed with onion, red pepper, parsley and garlic, to *Chipirones* (small squid served in a sauce made from their ink), *Bacalao a la vasca* (the classic Spanish way of preparing dried cod), *Almejas a la marinera* (*moules à la marinière*) to hake, sole and halibut prepared in various ways. The *Paella* is so well-made that once having tried it, one is inclined to ask for nothing else; but this would be a pity, because the speciality of the house is *Kokotxas*, an entirely individual dish prepared only from part of the throat or 'cheek' of the hake.

Most visitors will choose from the fish; but the Parador also offers good steaks, veal, ham in port, and a range of egg and vegetable dishes, as well as attractive desserts.

Another excellent local restaurant is that of the Provincial Hostal de Jaizkibel, overlooking the sea from a hilltop a short distance to the west along the coast.

The Basque country is too wet to produce wine in any quantity and the carafe wine is not of the locality. The region does, however, make Chacolí, a slightly pétillant 'green wine'. The Biscayans drink it quickly —'*ha de tomarse de golpe*' ('it must be swallowed at a gulp')—and with the excellent fish from the Costa Cantabrica it can, at its somewhat steely best, be pleasant. It is not to be found either at the Parador or in the better hotels and to sample it one must try the small bars in the area of nearby San Sebastián or Bilbao.

KOKOTXAS

Kokotxas are strips cut from the 'cheek' of the hake, so that it takes numerous hake to provide sufficient. The dish is a great delicacy.
Olive oil
2 cloves garlic, finely chopped
Salt and pepper
1 tablespoon chopped parsley
7oz (200gm) *kokotxas* per person, clean and dry
The portions are prepared individually in *cazuelas* or fireproof casseroles.

Heat a little olive oil in a *cazuela* and fry the garlic until golden. Now add the *kokotxas* and parsley, shaking or stirring vigorously so that the fish does not stick, and seasoning to taste. During this operation a little gelatine separates, providing a savoury sauce. Cooking is complete after 5 or 6 minutes.

ALMEJAS A LA MARINERA
MUSSELS A LA MARINIERE
Serves 4
2lb (1kg) mussels

1 tablespoon chopped parsley
½ bay leaf
½ glass dry white wine
Olive oil
1 onion, chopped
1 tablespoon breadcrumbs
1 clove of garlic
Juice of ½ lemon
1 teaspoon freshly ground black pepper
Salt

Scrape and wash the mussels, then put them in a saucepan with ½ pint
(¼ litre) of cold water. Cook briskly until they open, then remove them
and put them in another saucepan. Strain the water in which they have
been cooked through a cloth to remove sand and reserve.

Heat 3 fluid ounces (1dl) of olive oil and fry the onion and garlic
until golden, add the breadcrumbs, continue cooking briefly, then stir
in the reserved stock, the wine, bay leaf, lemon juice and black pepper
and bring to the boil. Pour this sauce over the mussels, simmer for
another 10 minutes, and season with the parsley and a little salt.

PAELLA MARINERA
In Valencia, where *Paella* originated, this saffron-tinted rice dish is
made with chicken, meat and small sausages; it has now become one of
the national dishes of Spain and may be made to perfection wherever
shellfish are abundant, as along the Cantabrian coast. The best cooking
vessel is a two-handled metal *paellera*, but a deep, good-sized frying
pan will serve very well.
Serves 6 to 8
2 poussins or a chicken of 2 to 3lb (1 to 1½kg)
Flour
Olive oil
1lb (½kg) small inkfish (squid)
2 pints (1kg) mussels
Rice (1 teacup per person)
Pinch saffron
Garlic
Shellfish—prawns, crayfish, lobster, crab, etc.
1 large can red peppers, cut in strips
Green or black olives

Inkfish is an important ingredient and when cut up and distributed in
the rice will not be noticed by people who otherwise fight shy of it.
Take your choice of the other shellfish. It may be fresh or frozen; but
preserved mussels are *not* suitable, since the vinegar ruins the flavour
of the finished dish.

Cut up the chicken, dredge with flour and brown lightly in hot olive
oil until tender. Put on a plate and reserve.

Clean the inkfish or get your fishmonger to do it. Cut it in small
pieces, fry in olive oil and put aside on another plate.

Scrape, clean and boil the mussels (see preceding recipe). Remove
them from the shells, keeping the best halves for decoration. Strain the
broth through muslin to remove grit and sand and keep for further use.

188

Put 2 tablespoons of olive oil into the *paellera* and fry 2 or 3 slices from a clove of garlic. When the garlic begins to brown, remove and discard it. Add the rice—preferably Spanish or Italian round rice and not the fluffy white, long-grained variety—in the proportion of 1 cupful per person. Fry gently until the rice begins to brown.

Meanwhile grind together in a mortar a clove of garlic and a pinch of saffron. Scatter over the fried rice.

The total amount of liquid required for boiling the rice is two cupfuls per person, i.e. exactly twice the amount of rice by volume, made up from the strained mussel stock plus as much additional water as is needed. Add this now, stirring for 5 minutes as it begins to bubble and boil through the rice.

Stir in the inkfish and arrange the pieces of chicken around the outside of the pan in a circle.

When the rice, inkfish and chicken have cooked together for about 15 minutes, add the remainder of the ingredients decoratively on top of this mixture: first the various cooked shellfish, then strips of red pepper and the green or black olives.

Finally, garnish with the mussels, replaced in the best of the half-shells in which they were cooked.

Turn off the heat and keep the *paella* covered with a clean teacloth for about 7 minutes, when it will be ready to serve. The *paellera* may be brought to the dinner table with dramatic effect; but if you are using a frying pan, the dish is served on individual dinner plates.

The once vigorous Hapsburg dynasty came to an end in 1700 with the childless, near-imbecile Charles II, the end result of generations of inbreeding. Louis XIV of France immediately laid claim to the Spanish throne in the person of his grandson, but the other European powers at once reacted to the possibility of an ultimate union of France and Spain under the Bourbons. The ensuing War of the Spanish Succession split Europe into two camps, with Spain and France on one side and a Grand Alliance of Britain, Austria, Holland and other countries on the other. Spain, too, was divided, since the Catalans seized the opportunity to reassert their claim to local autonomy and sided with the Allies.

General recognition of the Bourbon candidate, Philip V, as King of Spain after the treaty of Utrecht in 1713 ushered in the period of 'Enlightened Despotism', which lasted through the eighteenth century. The Bourbon monarchs, advised by intellectuals like Gaspar Melchor de Jovellanos, carried through many reforms. Abolition of Andalusia's monopoly of trade with America stimulated a great expansion of trade and commerce, especially in Catalonia. If social integration and a great increase in population were accompanied by a somewhat rigid centralization alien to the Spanish character and by widespread discontent over agrarian policies and the survival of many of the great land holdings, the Bourbons did succeed in rejuvenating Spanish power in Europe and America.

Casa del Barón: Pontevedra

The more settled conditions of the eighteenth century saw a change in the style of domestic architecture. The aristocrats no longer found it necessary to build fortified palaces in the guise of castles, with defensive towers and outworks. In Galicia the new style of baronial dwelling was known as a *Pazo*, of which a splendid example is the Parador of the Casa del Barón at Pontevedra in the far north-west of Spain.

It seems that the Pazo de Maceda, as it was originally known, was built on the site of a Roman villa. It underwent repeated reconstruction, notably in the sixteenth and early seventeenth centuries, when the fourth Count of Maceda, don Benito de Lanzos, remodelled it as a typical Galician *pazo*. When the line of the Macedas died out towards the end of the eighteenth century,

The courtyard of the Parador of the Casa del Barón, typical of a Galician *pazo*.

the house came into the possession of don Baltasar Pardo, Marquess of Figueroa and Atalaya. The Marquess played a distinguished part in the Peninsular War, commanding the famous Regiment of Saragossa. In July 1808 he fought under the ill-starred General Cuesta, who rashly challenged the forces of Marshal Bessières on open ground near the town of Medina de Río Seco, and lost his life in the ensuing rout which left the road to Madrid open to Joseph Bonaparte. After the death of its seigneur, the palace suffered many vicissitudes, becoming in turn a school, warehouse, masonic lodge and old people's home before passing to the Barons of Casa Goda, who meticulously restored and furnished it. On the death of the last of the Barons, it was acquired by the municipality and later by M.I.T.

The facade is neo-classical, and the interior, with its magnificent Baroque stairway, is typical of the traditional *pazo*. Another interesting feature is the old kitchen or *lar* in traditional Galician style.

Pontevedra, the Duo Pontes of the Romans, lies near the mouth of the River Lérez, one of the numerous and beautiful *Rías Bajas* of Galicia. It is a town of narrow streets, baronial houses and old churches. Next door is the thriving seaport of Vigo, one of Spain's main outlets to the Atlantic. It is also a convenient base for a visit to Santiago de Compostela and its great cathedral, which is within easy driving distance.

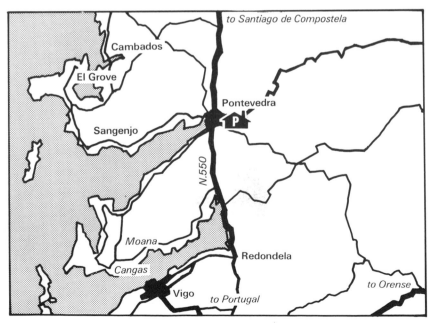

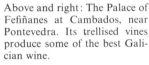
Above and right: The Palace of Fefiñanes at Cambados, near Pontevedra. Its trellised vines produce some of the best Galician wine.

Close as it is to the sea, the Parador, like those of Bayona and Villalba, specializes in seafood. Here, in season, one may eat *ostras* (oysters), *vieiras* (scallops) in their shells, *lamprea* (lamprey), *centollos* (spider crabs), *lubrigante* (lobster), *almejas* (clams) and *berberechos* (razor fish), which are served in a *salpicón* of mixed shellfish or in the shell with mayonnaise. Although it is perhaps rather strong for foreign tastes, octopus, fresh or dried, is a feature of the menu. The *Pulpo seco* (dried octopus) is cooked in large copper vessels and served in wooden bowls, seasoned with coarse sea-salt, paprika and olive oil. An excellent dish is the *Merluza a la gallega* (Galician-style hake), served in earthenware *cazuelas* with a sauce containing *chorizo* and potatoes spiced with paprika. The veal, beef and pork are all good, and are used in making one of the many variants of *Empanada gallega* (see page 119).

The best accompaniment to the Parador's seafood is the local *vino verde*, which is very similar to the better-known *vinho verde* ('green' or young wine) from Portugal.

It is somewhat surprising that Galicia, although one of the wettest districts of Spain, is one of the country's most prolific wine-growing areas. The vineyards line the steep slopes, and the vines are trained high from the ground on wires strung from chestnut stakes or granite pillars. Since the grapes receive less sunlight than in the south they contain less sugar and more malic acid (always present in unripe fruit), and undergo a 'secondary fermentation', which breaks down this excess acid and leaves them with an attractive, short-lived sparkle.

193

The principal wine-growing areas of Valdeorras, Monterrey, Orense and Ribeiro are all near Pontevedra and produce attractive white wines, low in alcohol and with a flowery bouquet, and astringent reds, perhaps best left to the Galicians. The largest producer is the Bodega Cooperativa de Ribeiro at Ribadavia, whose best wines are sold under the name of *Pazo* throughout the region and are available as far afield as Madrid and Soho.

Perhaps the best of all the Galician wines are the Albariños (named after the grape from which they are made) from Fefiñanes on the outskirts of the small port of Cambados to the north. These may be sampled in the pleasant modern Parador del Albariño in Cambados or in greater variety at the *Fiesta del Albariño*, held in the town during mid-August.

The local bodegas also make a potent spirit called *aguardiente*, akin to *Marc de Bourgogne*, by distilling the skins and pips of the grapes. To temper its strength the Galicians often set fire to it in a chinaware cup or prepare a more elaborate *Queimada* (from the Spanish *quemar*, to burn) by pouring half a bottle into an earthenware *cazuela* and adding roasted coffee beans, chunks of fresh lemon and maraschino cherries before setting light to the liquid.

Apart from the more expensive bottled wines, the Parador at Pontevedra offers a pleasant and inexpensive *vino verde* in carafes.

194

CENTOLLO A LA GALLEGA
SPIDER CRAB GALICIAN STYLE
Serves 1

Spider crabs differ from the British variety in possessing a flatter body and longer, more slender legs. They are plentiful—but no longer cheap —along the whole Atlantic coast of Spain.

1 spider crab (boiled)
½oz (15gm) butter
1 tablespoon brandy
Juice of 1 lemon
2 tablespoons dry white wine
1 tablespoon parsley, chopped
Freshly ground black pepper
Salt

Clean the spider crab as you would an ordinary crab, taking care to remove and discard the 'dead men's fingers'.

Take off the top shell from the body and scoop out the meat, putting it in a pan with the butter. Gently sauté, then pour on the brandy and flambé. Add the lemon juice, white wine and parsley and simmer slowly for about 10 minutes. Season to taste and put the mixture back into the crab, replacing the top shell to serve. Since spider crabs are not large, it is usual to serve one per person.

Right: The Cathedral at Santiago de Compostela near Pontevedra. The shrine of St. James in the cathedral was the goal of mediaeval pilgrims.

195

Charles III, the third of Spain's Bourbon rulers, who died in 1788, was an enlightened despot. He achieved many useful reforms: country tracks began to give way to modern roads radiating from Madrid; a much-needed overhaul of the top-heavy Spanish administration of the overseas empire led to an improvement in trade with America; an attempt was made to stimulate agriculture; schools, universities and hospitals were built; and courageous efforts were made to curb the power of the Church and Inquisition. His son, Charles IV, was an amiable but foolish man, more devoted to hunting than affairs of state, which were left to his masterful wife, María Luisa of Parma, and her favourite, Manuel Godoy. Under this unholy trinity, Spain lurched from one crisis to another and succeeded in antagonizing both Napoleon and her future ally, England. Enfeebled as the country was, it was more or less inevitable that Napoleon should invade the Peninsula, if only because it was the final and logical step in completing his Continental System and denying the arch-enemy, Britain, the last of her trading facilities.

The ensuing Peninsular War, which broke out in 1808 and raged for some five years, devastated the country and left it scarred and mutilated for years to come. That the French were finally driven out was largely due to the invincible spirit of the great mass of ordinary Spaniards, which took tangible shape in the incessant attack of the guerrillas on Napoleon's supply lines and garrisons, and to the brilliant military victories of a British soldier of genius, the Duke of Wellington.

Enrique II: Ciudad Rodrigo

In recognition of his services, Wellington was created Duke of Ciudad Rodrigo in 1812 after his capture of the fortress, now the Parador of Enrique II. Ciudad Rodrigo occupies a strategic position on the River Agueda on one of the main routes from Spain into northern Portugal. For the larger part of the war, Wellington's main base was in Portugal; and when in May 1810 Napoleon despatched Marshal Massena to drive the British into the sea, Ciudad Rodrigo was the target of the first onslaught. Under its gallant septuagenarian governor, General Errasti, the fortress held out against overwhelming odds until it was overrun by Marshal Ney two months later. Wellington meanwhile fell back on the Lines of Torres Vedras near Lisbon, luring Massena's army to its destruction. When the Duke mounted his great counter-offensive in January 1812, his first step was to secure Ciudad Rodrigo. His troops cut zig-zags in the frozen ground, moved up to the walls and

The Parador of Enrique II, seen from the River Agueda.

Below: The Monastery of Nuestra Sra. della Peña de Francia on its mountain peak near the mediaeval village of La Alberca.

burst through a couple of breaches. The great moat and walls, stormed with such cruel loss to the attackers, have survived intact; and it is possible to make the round of the town along the broad encompassing ramparts.

During the murderous bombardments of the war the castle was reduced to a shattered ruin, but it has since been carefully restored

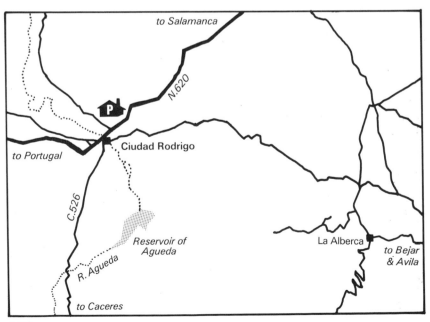

198

and conserves many of its mediaeval features, such as the great central keep, the flanking walls and ramparts, the courtyard and some of the great interior chambers.

The site was first fortified in Roman times, but the present building dates back to the reign of Ferdinand II of León at the end of the twelfth century. It subsequently saw incessant fighting. Ciudad Rodrigo earned privileges from Henry of Trastámara by taking his side in his rebellion against Pedro the Cruel a century later, and was the base for various expeditions against Portugal. When the Hapsburg dynasty came to an end in 1700, the castle was captured by the unsuccessful Austrian claimant to the throne, the Archduke Charles, after fierce fighting with the Duke of

Berwick, but was subsequently repossessed by the first of the Spanish Bourbons, Philip V. A worn inscription over its arched Gothic entrance testifies to a mediaeval past.

> *The construction of this castle was ordered by the most high and noble king don Enrique, son of the most high and noble king don Alonso, who defeated Alboacen, King of Benamarin with all the strength of Africa and won Algecira. Work began on the first day of June 1410.*

The little walled town of Ciudad Rodrigo is one of the most unspoilt in Spain and has been declared a National Monument. Its beautiful cathedral dates from the twelfth century; and off its narrow streets there are many noble baronial houses with interior patios. In this age of the impersonal supermarket, just to browse round its shops is to journey back into the traditional Spain: one cavernous, wooden-floored emporium abruptly changes from a grocer's to a shoe shop, with the *chorizos* and hams side by side with serried boxes of footware.

Ciudad Rodrigo lies in an open expanse dotted with cork oaks; to the southeast is the remote and beautiful Sierra de Francia, range upon range of mountains clothed in oak and chestnut, with the occasional orchard or vineyard clinging to the steep slopes. In the heart of this wilderness, until recently almost unapproachable by car, but now an easy hour's drive from the Parador, is the remarkable mediaeval village of La Alberca, a place of granite houses with their upper floors built out on wooden baulks and overhanging the narrowest of streets, paved with cobbles and flagstones. Writing as recently as 1960, Sacheverell Sitwell remarks, 'It is difficult to indicate the degree of darkness of the side alleys, but already one dreads the thought of La Alberca after nightfall. . . . Looking out from a window, before dinner in the castle-Parador, more than ever like a fortress now that we had returned to its safe shelter from La Alberca, a wild rain was sweeping over the huge plain towards Portugal. It blew and shook the windows, it rattled at the doors. This keep or bastion in the town walls stood out in the wild weather with such an isolation that you felt you were on a ship at sea . . .'

If the waitresses in the Parador's dining room do not boast the velvet, lace, gold galloon, coral beads and silver buttons, worn not so long ago in La Alberca, their costume is still eye-catching. A red and white striped skirt is topped by a white blouse and black sash, over which they wear a short black bodice trimmed with green ribbon and laced in white at the front. White stockings and black shoes complete this colourful garb.

In Sitwell's time, because of the difficulty of supply, 'there was little but eggs and chicken to be had from nearby,' but the Parador's menu,

Above: A peasant from the village of La Alberca in traditional costume with silver buttons.

Opposite: A house in La Alberca, near Ciudad Rodrigo.

200

if not one of the most extensive, is now varied enough. The region is famous for its cured hams and sausages; and the local *chorizo*, a pork sausage spiced with pimiento, may be sampled in the excellent *entremeses* (hors d'oeuvres), which as usual run to some dozen and a half separate dishes. The dark, highly-cured ham may be eaten on its own, thinly-sliced with a salad or in *Heuvos revueltos con jamón*, an entirely individual Spanish variation of scrambled eggs. The *Tortilla paisana* (country omelette), cooked like a pancake, also contains this ham, together with peas, potato and red peppers. The trout, fished locally, is fresh and good; and among the best of the meat dishes are the *Magras de cerdo en cazuela*, fillets of pork served in earthenware casseroles with a tomato sauce.

    This northern stretch of the Portuguese marches is not wine-growing country, but the Parador serves acceptable carafe wine and a range of Riojas for those who demand something more sophisticated.

TORTILLA PAISANA
COUNTRY OMELETTE
Serves 2
1 large potato
1 onion
Olive oil
Salt and pepper
3 to 4 eggs
2oz (60gm) cooked garden peas
2oz (60gm) *jamón serrano* or ordinary cooked ham cut into strips
2oz (60gm) red peppers, either cooked or from a can, and cut into strips
Cut up the potato and onion and fry slowly in olive oil for 10 minutes, seasoning with salt and pepper. Remove with a draining spoon and reserve. Beat the eggs in a bowl, add all the other ingredients and check the seasoning. Clean the frying pan, then pour back a little of the oil and heat it until it just begins to smoke. Pour in the egg mixture and cook on one side for a minute or two, then slide the omelette on to a plate, cooked side downwards. Place another plate on top and invert it.

202

With the uncooked side now downwards, slide the omelette back into the pan and cook for another 2 or 3 minutes. Alternatively, if you find it easier, put a plate on top of the frying pan and reverse it, as described on page 29. The finished omelette looks like a pancake.

MAGRAS DE CERDO EN CAZUELA
FILLETS OF PORK IN TOMATO SAUCE
Serves 3
Olive oil
1 onion, chopped
1lb ($\frac{1}{2}$kg) loin of pork or a cut from the leg in the form of small round *medaillons*
Flour
1 clove of garlic
1 tablespoon chopped parsley
$\frac{1}{2}$lb (225gm) tomatoes, blanched or from a can
$\frac{1}{2}$ teaspoon castor sugar
Salt and pepper
Heat a little olive oil in a frying pan and cook the onion for about 15 minutes until golden. Pour off the oil, then add the garlic, parsley and tomatoes and simmer for about 10 minutes. Season with sugar, salt and pepper and either rub the cooked ingredients through a sieve or put into a blender to make a smooth sauce.

Meanwhile dredge the fillets of pork in flour and fry in a little olive oil to brown them. Drain and place in a casserole with the sauce and cook gently for 30 minutes.

Right: A Baroque window in the Cathedral of Ciudad Rodrigo.

203

The Peninsular War cast forward long shadows across the Spanish history of the nineteenth century. When the 'Desired One', Ferdinand VII, returned to Spain in 1814 after his long exile in France, his authoritarian policies split the country and were indirectly responsible for the loss of the American colonies. Before his death in 1833, he remarked that 'Spain is a bottle of beer and I am the cork. Without me it would all go off in froth.' His prediction was only too near the mark.

The first Carlist War of 1833–40 and the subsequent uprisings of 1846–48 and 1872 had their origin in his rejection of the Salic Law, which provided that a woman might never succeed to the throne of Spain. The law had been repealed in 1789, but the decision was not made public until forty years later. If Queen Cristina had borne Ferdinand a son, there could have been no argument about the succession; as it was, both of his children were girls, and Ferdinand's brother, Don Carlos, refused to recognize the Infanta Isabel as heir to the throne.

What made the ensuing war so bitter was that it was more than a dynastic struggle. Although the regent, Queen Cristina, was no whole-hearted reformer, she was compelled to fall back on the support of the 'liberals', themselves deeply divided between 'moderates' and 'progressives'. Don Carlos was a devout and convinced Catholic and was supported by the extreme 'apostolic' party, which fiercely resented the erosion of the Church's political influence and the waning powers of the Inquisition. The Carlists also gained support from the Basques, whose primary object was to protect their local rights and institutions against encroachment from Madrid. Their weakness was that they never succeeded in taking over any of the major centres of population, and throughout seven years of guerrilla warfare remained strongest in the country districts.

Cardenal Ram: Morella

A main Carlist bastion during the latter part of the war was the mediaeval town of Morella in the mountain fastness of the Maestrazgo, lying back from the Mediterranean to the northeast of Valencia and Castellón de la Plana and now the site of the Provincial Parador of Cardenal Ram.

With its stout mediaeval walls and its fortress, crowning the great rock which rears up in the centre of the town, Morella was a prize for both sides. To begin with the townspeople declared for the Cristino or government party, but as the Carlist leader Ramón Cabrera built up his forces in the inaccessible mountains of the

The entrance of the Parador of Cardenal Ram.

205

Maestrazgo, the Carlists made various attempts to capture it. All were unsuccessful until a deserter from the garrison, Ramón Orgué, approached the commander of one of the Carlist detachments blockading the town. His plan was to gain access by means of ladders to a privy used by the garrison, to remove the wooden seat and so to penetrate the castle walls. It was judged so hazardous that volunteers were called for. On the dark and stormy night of 25 January 1838, some twenty Carlists successfully entered the precinct of the fortress and by raising shouts of 'Viva Cabrera! Viva Carlos V!' panicked the garrison and governor into surrender.

The loss of Morella, after the defeat of the main Carlist forces and the death of General Zumalacárregui in the north, was a serious blow to the Cristinos. An army under General Oraá was despatched to recapture it and breached the walls, but was cut off from its supplies by Cabrera and forced to retire. Morella then became the Carlist headquarters; and Cabrera's black flag, with its white skull and crossbones, floated above the fortress until its recapture by General Espartero in May, 1840, ended the war.

The battles of the Carlist Wars were only the penultimate episode

Above: General Ramón Cabrera y Griño, who seized Morella from the Government forces and made it his headquarters during the latter stages of the Carlist Wars.

Below: A gun from the Carlist Wars at the Castle of Morella.

of a warlike past stretching back to Celtiberian times. The invading vandals fought over Morella with the Romans; it was captured by the Moors in 714 and taken from them by El Cid in 1086, who made it his base prior to his capture of Valencia and on its wooded approaches defeated Count Berenguer Ramón II of Barcelona at the famous battle of El Pinar de Tevar. It was finally repossessed on behalf of the Christians by James the Conqueror of Aragon-Catalonia in 1232 and played its part on the European stage, when in 1414 it was the scene for a meeting between a king, Ferdinand of Antequera; a saint, Vincente de Ferrer; and a Pope.

Pedro de Luna, in their attempt to heal the rift between the Popes of Rome and Avignon.

Some of the bloodiest episodes in its history occurred during the Peninsular War, when its streets rang to the sound of firing squads, as the French garrison took its revenge on the inhabitants for lending support to the guerrillas in their rash attempts to retake it.

The Parador is one of numerous noble seignorial houses lying off the narrow, hilly streets and was the residence of Cardenal Ram, a counsellor of Ferdinand of Antequera, who became king of Aragon-Catalonia after the last of the Counts of Barcelona died in 1410.

The most eye-catching of Morella's sights is the enormous castle, towering above the town, its fortifications linking with the encircling walls, which date from the fourteenth century and are pierced by four battlemented gates. The approach to the battle-scarred fortress is by a wide and lengthy ramp, winding around the hill and flanked at each level by enfilading walls. A cannon from the Carlist Wars still points skyward; and from the top there is an immense vista of the sierra, with the houses and blue dome of the Church of Santa María doll-like below. The church, begun in 1273, with its beautiful

208

carvings of the Apostles over the entrance and extraordinary churriguresque altar-piece, embodying a portrait of James the Conqueror by Ribalta, is not to be missed. A small museum, forming the gatehouse of the castle, houses relics dating from prehistoric times and also an interesting exhibition relating to the folklore and domestic arts of the Maestrazgo. A kilometre or so from the town the mountain road to Alcañiz passes beneath one of the arches of a lofty aqueduct, described by local historians as mediaeval, but probably Moorish in origin; and further afield at Morella la Vella, there are rock shelters decorated with palaeolithic and neolithic paintings of hunting and war.

Opposite: An aqueduct, probably of Moorish origin, on the outskirts of Morella. Below: The town and its encircling wall and castle (from a nineteenth-century engraving).

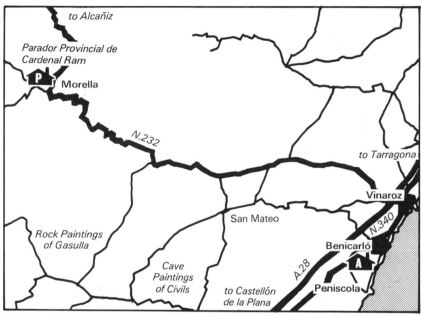

The region produces excellent *embutidos* (cured meats and salami), including *cecina* and *somarro*, dried and salted beef and mutton, perhaps best sampled in the *entremeses* (hors d'oeuvres) rather than as dishes on their own. The lamb is first-rate; and the Parador serves an excellent *Cordero lechal asado* (roast milk-fed lamb). The local mushrooms are of a flavour almost forgotten in these days of the mass-produced button variety; and there are numerous good cheeses—that of Troncho merited mention in *Don Quixote*. Like many towns once occupied by the Moors, Morella makes a variety of delicious sweetmeats and small cakes, usually with a basis of almonds and sugar.

The Parador of Cardenal Ram, like the Hostal of Jaizkibel (see page 187), is run by the Provincial authorities and not by M.I.T. This, on occasion, results in somewhat amateur but endearing service—as, for example, when an extremely youthful waiter served two large wine glasses of brandy after lunch! Although comparatively near the sea, the mountainous Maestrazgo is an enclave on its own; and its cooking is not representative of the Levante in general, with its profusion of seafood and rice dishes.

209

There are local wines from Valderrobles and Calenda; but your carafe will probably hail from Benicarló on the coast, whose dark, strong red wines were once in so much demand for blending with the thinner brews of northern Europe.

Below: Cave drawings found near Morella (after a drawing by J. Pascual).

SETAS CON AJO Y PEREJIL
MUSHROOMS WITH GARLIC AND PARSLEY
In Spain the large 'mushrooms' displayed for sale in the markets are different from both the button or field varieties familiar in Britain, but they may be bought and eaten with confidence.
Serves 2
2oz (60gm) pork fat
½lb (250gm) mushrooms, cleaned but not washed
3 cloves of garlic
4 tablespoons chopped parsley
Salt and pepper
Heat the pork fat in a pan, add the mushrooms, squeeze the garlic over them, add the parsley and cook slowly for 10 minutes, turning them at intervals. Serve hot straight from the pan.

Left: Thunderstorms over Morella, with the tiled dome of the Church of Santa María la Mayor in the foreground.

CHURROS

By this point in his travels the visitor may well be tiring of the standard Continental breakfast, which only too often consists of bread reheated from the day before, sweet *confituras* and rather solid cakes. The answer is *churros*, golden brown fingers served hot from the smoking olive oil in which they are cooked, and available at most of the Paradores. They may be made at home if one acquires the special forcing tube—obtainable for a few pesetas from any Spanish ironmonger.

18fl oz (8.5dl) water
2/3oz (20gm) salt
14oz (400gm) flour
2 eggs
Olive oil
A little castor sugar

Put the water and salt to boil in a large saucepan, add the flour and salt, and stir vigorously with a wooden spoon. Remove the pan from the heat when the paste begins to stick to the sides. Add the eggs and beat until a stiff ball is formed—like choux pastry.

Heat some olive oil in a pan; when it begins smoking it is hot enough to fry the *churros*. Fill the forcing tube with the dough and express long dollops, about the size and shape of a chipolata sausage, into the oil. Fry until they are dark golden, remove with a draining spoon, powder with sugar and serve with all speed.

Right: The carved roof of the Parador of Cardenal Ram, once the palace of the fifteenth-century Cardenal Ram.

211

General Baldomero Espartero's success in concluding the first Carlist War emboldened him to force Queen Cristina's resignation as regent and to take over the government of the country in the name of the Progressives. He was himself soon deposed and for the long period until 1868 the country was ruled by Moderate governments. Their fall brought down the monarchy with it. The First Republic lasted for eleven months from February, 1873, to January, 1874, when the Bourbon dynasty was restored in the person of Alfonso XII.

These convulsions corresponded to profound changes in the social and economic life of the country. The latter years of the nineteenth century saw a great expansion of commerce and manufacture in Catalonia and the development of heavy industry along the Cantabrian coast, based on its coal and iron deposits. With this came the emergence of an urban proletariat, which was quick to take part in the growth of a general European socialist movement. Especially in Catalonia, anarchist groups appeared, devoted to the overthrow of the bourgeois world by acts of violence; and between 1892 and 1897 Barcelona was the scene of repeated acts of terrorism, which were the curtain-raiser to the street warfare of 1917–22. Added to this were radical changes in the role of the Catholic Church, the running sore of unpopular wars in Morocco and the disaster of the Spanish-American War, which resulted in the loss of the Spanish West Indies and the Philippines. Spain was clearly ripe for a dictatorship of the right or left; and a period of authoritarian government by General Primo de Rivera from 1923–29 gave way to the establishment of the Second Republic in April 1931.

Gredos: Gredos

King Alfonso XIII, who left the country at this point to avert the danger of civil war, will be remembered, among matters of greater import, for his part in founding the Parador of Gredos, the first of the present network. An enthusiastic huntsman, it was he who in 1926 chose the panoramic site at the top of the 1,650m Pass of Risquillo in the Sierra de Gredos south of Avila. He opened the Parador in 1928.

The Parador was constructed as a roomy hunting lodge; and it was not only King Alfonso who used it to hunt the rare *Capra hispanica*: in one of the lounges there is a photograph of a youthful General Franco surrounded by the trophies of the chase. The fishing of salmon trout in the River Tormes is another of its attractions. The Parador, within easy reach of Madrid, soon proved so popular as a haven from urban noise and tension that it was extended in 1941 and again in 1975. For most of its visitors its principal charms are the unbroken silence of the mountains, the long view from the terrace of the high sierra, the all-pervading fragrance of pine, and the shaded walks in the surrounding forest. In the fall these forest rides are starred with the purple of the autumn crocus.

The Parador of Gredos as it looked before the extensions undertaken in 1975.

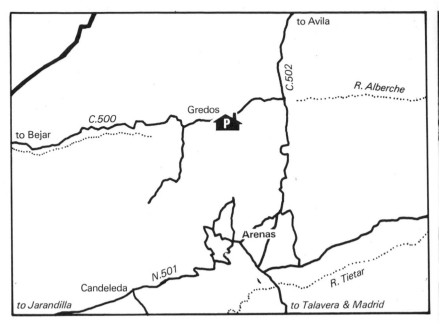

The Parador is on no direct route, but the mountain road, which follows the winding upland course of the Tormes from Avila, eventually joins the main route from Madrid to Badajoz and Portugal within a kilometre of the Parador at Oropesa; and Gredos is an even more convenient starting point for the excursions from Avila already described (see page 171).

Above: A lounge in the Parador of Gredos. The hunting trophies are of the famous *Capra hispánica*. Left: The Parador's balcony overlooking the Sierra de Gredos.

Right: The Parador as it looks today.

The Parador's cooking is sophisticated, as befits its clientele. Trout from the River Tormes is available in various forms: with ham (see page 45), marinated, and perhaps most delicious of all, freshly smoked on the premises over Danish wood chips immediately prior to serving. Other specialities are *Migas* (fried breadcrumbs, see page 46) served either with eggs or fillets of pork; *Judias del Barco con oreja y chorizo* (chick peas stewed with pig's ear and *chorizo*); lamb and kid, either roast or in the form of a *Caldereta* (see page 168); ribs of beef; *Estofado de ternera* (ragout of veal); game in season; and, as a sweet, the *Yemas de Santa Teresa* (see page 173) so typical of the region.

The local red wine from Cebreros, containing a hefty 16 per cent alcohol, is available in carafe or bottled under the name of 'El Galayo'.

CODORNICES A LA CASERA
ROAST QUAIL
Serves 2
2 quail
2oz (60gm) pork fat
2oz (60gm) cooked ham, cut up
1 teaspoon mixed herbs
Salt and pepper
1 large glass dry white wine
6 shallots or spring onions
2oz (60gm) mushrooms
5fl oz ($1\frac{1}{2}$dl) stock
Put the quail in a roasting tin surrounded by the other ingredients, finally pouring in the wine and stock. Preheat the oven and roast at moderate heat (375°F, Mark 5) for $\frac{1}{2}$ hour, basting at intervals.

Above: The Castle of Mombeltran near Gredos, once the seat of the Dukes of Alburquerque.

Left: The village of Mombeltran.

TOCINO DE CIELO

Quaintly translated as 'Salt Pork from Heaven' in some Parador menus, this is in fact a traditional dessert.

12 eggs
1lb (½kg) castor sugar
9fl oz (2.5dl) water
1 vanilla pod

Rub the eggs through a sieve. Simmer 12oz (140gm) of the sugar in a saucepan in the water, together with the vanilla pod, until the syrup thickens to the point when a spoon dipped into it trails long strands.

Add the egg mixture to the syrup little by little, stirring all the time. Meanwhile prepare some caramel by heating the remaining 4oz (110gm) of sugar with a little water until it begins to darken, and use this to coat a mould. Pour in the contents of the saucepan, cover with foil, and cook in a Bain Marie or large saucepan of boiling water for 10 minutes. Allow to cool and then turn out on to a serving dish.

Right: Maite Manjón at the door of the Church of Santa María la Mayor, Morella.

4 Gazetteer: where to stay and eat

Paradores, Albergues, Hosterías and Refugios open Autumn 1976

Information is given in the following order: place and province; name and category; telephone number; double and single rooms; and type of building.

PARADORES

AIGUABLAVA (Gerona)
PARADOR NACIONAL COSTA BRAVA****
972 312162; 72 and 8; new building by the sea

ALARCON (Cuenca)
PARADOR NACIONAL MARQUES DE VILLENA***
966 331350; 10 and 1; castle in the country

ALBACETE (Albacete)
PARADOR NACIONAL LA MANCHA****
967 214290; 67 and 3; new building in the country

ALCAÑIZ (Teruel)
PARADOR NACIONAL LA CONCORDIA****
974 130400; 10 and 2; palace in town

ARCOS DE LA FRONTERA (Cádiz)
PARADOR NACIONAL CASA DEL CORREGIDOR****
056 362; 18 and 3; new building in town

AVILA (Ávila)
PARADOR NACIONAL RAIMUNDO DE BORGOÑA***
918 211340; 26 and 1; palace in town

AYAMONTE (Huelva)
PARADOR NACIONAL COSTA DE LA LUZ****
955 320700; 19 and 1; new building by the sea

BAYONA (Pontevedra)
PARADOR NACIONAL CONDE DE GONDOMAR****
086 142; 108 and 20; historic building by the sea

BENAVENTE (Zamora)
PARADOR NACIONAL REY FERNANDO II DE LEON****
988 630300; 28 and 2; castle in town

BIELSA (Huesca)
PARADOR NACIONAL MONTE PERDIDO****
074 23; 15 and 1; new building in the mountains

CALAHORRA (Logroño)
PARADOR NACIONAL MARCO FABIO QUINTILIANO****
941 130358; 61 and 6; new building in town

CAMBADOS (Pontevedra)
PARADOR NACIONAL DEL ALBARIÑO***
086 171; 8 double rooms only; new building by the sea

LAS CAÑADAS DEL TEIDE (Canaries)
PARADOR NACIONAL CAÑADAS DEL TEIDE***
Radio telephone; 25 and 2; new building in the mountains

CAZORLA (Jaén)
PARADOR NACIONAL DEL ADELANTADO***
053 295; 16 and 6; new building in the country

CUIDAD RODRIGO (Salamanca)
PARADOR NACIONAL ENRIQUE II***
923 460150; 16 and 12; castle in town

CORDOBA (Córdoba)
PARADOR NACIONAL LA ARRUZAFA****
957 275900; 54 and 2; new building in town

CRUZ DE TEJEDA (Canaries)
PARADOR NACIONAL CRUZ DE TEJEDA**
928 658050; 13 and 6; new building in the mountains

EL FERROL DEL CAUDILLO (La Coruña)
PARADOR NACIONAL EL FERROL DEL CAUDILLO***
981 353400; 22 and 5; new building in town

FUENTE DE (Santander)
PARADOR NACIONAL RIO DEVA****
042-Camaleno 7; 72 and 6; new building in the mountains

FUENTERRABIA (Guipúzcoa)
PARADOR NACIONAL EL EMPERADOR***
943 642140; 14 and 2; palace in town

FUENTES CARRIONAS (Zamora)
PARADOR NACIONAL FUENTES CARRIONAS****
988 870075; 72 and 8; new building in the mountains

GIJON (Oviedo)
PARADOR NACIONAL MOLINO VIEJO***
985 354945; 6 double rooms only; new building in town

GOMERA (Canaries)
PARADOR NACIONAL CONDE DE GOMERA***
922 871100; 19 and 1; new building by the beach

GRANADA (Granada)
PARADOR NACIONAL SAN FRANCISCO****
958 221462; 50 and 2; convent in the town

GREDOS (Ávila)
PARADOR NACIONAL GREDOS****
018-Barco de Avila 550; 75 and 4; new building in the mountains

GUADALUPE (Cáceres)
PARADOR NACIONAL ZURBARAN***
027 142; 19 and 1; palace in town

JARANDILLA (Cáceres)
PARADOR NACIONAL CARLOS V***
027 98; 20 and 3; castle in town

JAVEA (Alicante)
PARADOR NACIONAL COSTA BLANCA****
965 790200; 57 and 3; new building by beach

MALAGA (Málaga)
PARADOR NACIONAL GIBRALFARO***
952 221902; 11 and 1; new building in town

MAZAGON (Huelva)
PARADOR NACIONAL CRISTOBAL COLON****
055 303; 19 and 1; new building by beach

MELILLA (Spanish Morocco)
PARADOR NACIONAL DON PEDRO ESTOPIÑAN****
952 684940; 25 and 2; new building in town

MERIDA (Badajoz)
PARADOR NACIONAL VIA DE LA PLATA****
924 301540; 44 and 1; convent in town

MOJACAR (Almeria)
PARADOR NACIONAL REYES CATOLICOS****
051 26; 90 and 9; new building by beach

MONACHIL (Granada)
PARADOR NACIONAL SIERRA NEVADA***
958 480200; 30 and 2; new building in the mountains

MONZON DE CAMPOS (Palencia)
PARADOR NACIONAL MONZON DE CAMPOS***
088 51; 8 and 2; castle in the country

NERJA (Málaga)
PARADOR NACIONAL NERJA****
952 520050; 38 and 2; new building by beach

OLITE (Navarra)
PARADOR NACIONAL PRINCIPE DE VIANA***
948 740000; 36 and 4; castle in town

OROPESA (Toledo)
PARADOR NACIONAL VIRREY DE TOLEDO****
025 172; 45 and 2; castle in town

PAJARES (Oviedo)
PARADOR NACIONAL PUERTO PAJARES***
985 473625; 24 and 6; new building in the mountains

PONTEVEDRA (Pontevedra)
PARADOR NACIONAL CASA DEL BARON***
986 855800; 45 and 2; palace in town

PUERTO DEL ROSARIO (Canaries)
PARADOR NACIONAL FUERTEVENTURA***
928 850075; 22 and 2; new building by beach

PUERTOMARIN (Lugo)
PARADOR NACIONAL PUERTOMARIN***
082 20; 9 and 1; new building in the country

RIBADEO (Lugo)
PARADOR NACIONAL RIBADEO****
982 110825; 41 and 6; new building by the sea

EL SALER (Valencia)
PARADOR NACIONAL LUIS VIVES****
963 236850; 38 and 2; new building by the beach

SANTA CRUZ DE LA PALMA (Canaries)
PARADOR NACIONAL SANTA CRUZ DE LA
PALMA***
922 412340; 11 and 17; new building in town

SANTILLANA (Santander)
PARADOR NACIONAL GIL BLAS***
042 116; 22 and 2; palace in town

SANTO DOMINGO DE LA CALZADA (Logroño)
PARADOR NACIONAL SANTO DOMINGO DE LA
CALZADA***
941 340300; 25 and 2; palace in town

SORIA (Soria)
PARADOR NACIONAL ANTONIO MACHADO***
975 213445; 13 and 1; new building in town

SOS DE REY CATOLICO (Navarra)
PARADOR NACIONAL FERNANDO DE ARAGON****
076 96; 60 and 6; new building in town

TERUEL (Teruel)
PARADOR NACIONAL DE TERUEL***
974 601800; 28 and 2; new building in town

TOLEDO (Toledo)
PARADOR NACIONAL CONDE DE ORGAZ****
925 221850; 22; new building in town

TORDESILLAS (Valladolid)
PARADOR NACIONAL TORDESILLAS****
083 514; 67 and 6; new building in the country

TORREMOLINOS (Málaga)
PARADOR NACIONAL DEL GOLF****
962 381120; 38 and 2; new building by beach

TUY (Pontevedra)
PARADOR NACIONAL SAN TELMO***
086 296; 15 and 1; new building in town

UBEDA (Jaén)
PARADOR NACIONAL CONDESTABLE DAVALOS***
953 750345; 24 and 1; palace in town

VERIN (Orense)
PARADOR NACIONAL MONTERREY***
988 410075; 22 and 1; new building in country

VICH (Barcelona)
PARADOR NACIONAL VICH****
093 241; 25 and 6; new building in country

VIELLA (Lérida)
PARADOR NACIONAL VALLE DE ARAN****
073 108; 115 and 19; new building in the mountains

VILLAFRANCA DEL BIERZO (León)
PARADOR NACIONAL VILLAFRANCA***
147; 32 and 9; new building on highway

VILLALBA (Lugo)
PARADOR NACIONAL CONDES DE VILLALBA***
982 296; 6 double rooms only; castle in town

ZAFRA (Badajoz)
PARADOR NACIONAL HERNAN CORTES****
924 550200; 22 and 6; castle in town

ZAMORA (Zamora)
PARADOR NACIONAL CONDES DE ALBA Y
ALISTE***
988 514497; 18 and 1; palace in town

ALBERGUES

ANTEQUERA (Málaga)
ALBERGUE NACIONAL DE ANTEQUERA*
952 841740; 15 and 2; new building on highway

ARANDA DEL DUERO (Burgos)
ALBERGUE NACIONAL DE ARANDA DE DUERO**
947 500050; 6 and 15; new building on highway

BAILEN (Jaén)
ALBERGUE NACIONAL DE BAILEN****
053 372; 38 and 2; new building on highway

LA BAÑEZA (León)
ALBERGUE NACIONAL ESCUELA DE LA BAÑEZA*
987 641850; 8 and 4; new building on highway

BENICARLO (Castellón de la Plana)
ALBERGUE NACIONAL DE BENICARLO****
964 470100; 93 and 15; new building by the sea

MANZANARES (Ciudad Real)
ALBERGUE NACIONAL DE MANZANARES**
926 610400; 11 and 20; new building on highway

PUEBLA DE SANABRIA (Zamora)
ALBERGUE NACIONAL PUEBLA DE SANABRIA***
988 620001; 10 and 14; new building on highway

PUERTO LUMBRERAS (Murcia)
ALBERGUE NACIONAL DE PUERTO LUMBRERAS**
968 402025; 11 and 2; new building on highway

SANTA MARIA DE HUERTA (Soria)
ALBERGUE NACIONAL SANTA MARIA DE
HUERTA****
675 20; 38 and 2; new building on highway

VILLACASTIN (Segovia)
ALBERGUE NACIONAL DE VILLACASTIN***
911 107000; 12 and 1; new building on highway

HOSTERIAS

ALCALA DE HENARES (Madrid)
HOSTERIA NACIONAL DEL ESTUDIANTE****
918 880330; no rooms; historic building in town

ARTIES (Lérida)
HOSTERIA NACIONAL DON GASPAR PORTOLA****
073 10; no rooms; castle in the country

CACERES (Cáceres)
HOSTERIA NACIONAL DEL COMENDADOR****
927 213012; no rooms; palace in town

PEDRAZA DE LA SIERRA (Segovia)
HOSTERIA NACIONAL PINTOR ZULOAGA****
011 15; no rooms; historic building in town

REFUGIO

OJEN (Málaga)
REFUGIO NACIONAL DE JUANAR***
952 826140; 8 and 1; new building in mountains

HOTEL

CADIZ (Cádiz)
HOTEL ATLANTICO****
956 212301; 51 double rooms only; new building in town

Index

Illustration Acknowledgements
The publishers are grateful to the following for supplying illustrations: Archiv General de Simancas: 131; Brinsley Ford, Esq.: 134; British Museum: 75 right, top, bottom; Foto Mas: 58 top, 71 top, 100 top, 101 top, 108, 114, 122 top, 129, 160 top, 168, 171 top, 178 bottom, 186, 187, 195; Foto Oronoz: 26, 94; Hispanic Council: 52, 69 top, middle left, bottom left, 88, 147, 166 top, 206 top, 208 bottom, 210; Ministerio de Información y Turismo: title page, 8, 24, 28 top, 32, 35, 37, 38, 40, 41, 43, 48, 50, 56, 57, 58 bottom, 60, 62, 64, 68, 71 bottom, 73, 77, 78, 79, 83 top, 85, 87, 89, 91, 92, 93, 96, 97, 99, 100 bottom, 102, 103 top, 104, 106, 111, 115, 116 top, 119, 120, 122 bottom, 124, 125, 128, 133, 135, 136, 139, 141, 146, 149, 150, 152, 155, 156, 157, 161, 164, 165, 167 right, 172, 173, 176 bottom, 177, 178 top, 179, 183, 185, 191, 194, 197, 202, 214 bottom, 215 top & bottom; National Portrait Gallery: 198 top; Prado Museum: 151; Jan Read: half-title page, 25, 27, 28 bottom, 34, 44, 45, 46, 53, 55, 65, 66, 70, 76, 82 right, 83 bottom, 103 bottom, 113, 116 bottom, 126, 127, 132, 143, 158, 159 bottom, 160 bottom, 162, 171 right, 175, 176 top, 181, 189, 192 top, 193, 199, 200, 201, 203, 205, 206 bottom, 207, 208 top, 210 top, 211, 213, 216, 217.

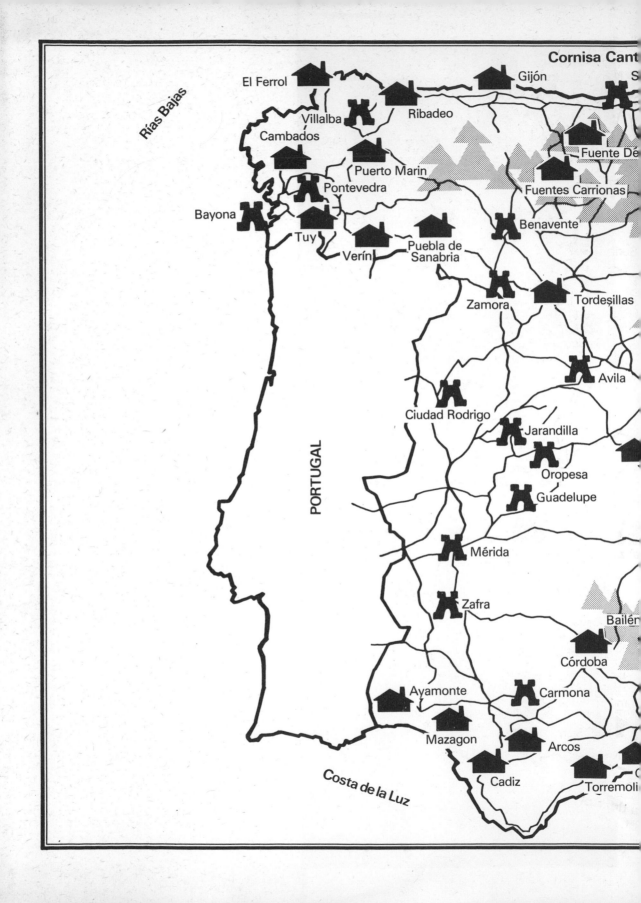